Major Donor Fundraising

Margaret Holman and Lucy Sargent

directory of social change

The fundraising series
For all titles available in this series see:
www.dsc.org.uk/fundraisingseries

Published by the Directory of Social Change (Registered Charity no. 800517 in England and Wales)

Head office: Resource for London, 352 Holloway Rd, London N7 6PA

Northern office: Suite 103, 1 Old Hall Street, Liverpool L3 9HG

Tel: 08450 77 77 07

Visit www.dsc.org.uk to find out more about our books, subscription funding websites and training events. You can also sign up for e-newsletters so that you're always the first to hear about what's new.

The publisher welcomes suggestions and comments that will help to inform and improve future versions of this and all of our titles. Please give us your feedback by emailing publications@dsc.org.uk.

It should be understood that this publication is intended for guidance only and is not a substitute for professional or legal advice. No responsibility for loss occasioned as a result of any person acting or refraining from acting can be accepted by the authors or publisher.

First published 2006 by the Directory of Social Change
Reprinted 2011, 2012, 2016

ISBN 978 1 903991 68 8

British Library Cataloguing in Publication Data
A catalogue record for this book is available from the British Library

Cover design by Kate Griffith
Original text design Eugenie Dodd Typographics
Typeset by Keystroke, Wolverhampton
Printed and bound by Page Bros, Norwich

Contents

Acknowledgements

We send our heartfelt thanks to the following individuals who contributed to the development of this publication by willingly sharing their practices, knowledge and expertise of major gift fundraising. Thanks so much to all of you.

Expert Panel Reviewers

- Finbar Cullen, ResearchPlus, UK

- Alison Goodman, Major Gift and Celebrity Manager, Terrence Higgins Trust, UK

- Brian Hanratty, Chief Executive Officer of GORTA, The Freedom from Hunger Council of Ireland, Eire

- Nina Botting Herbst, Associate Director of Development and Alumni Relations, Division of the Social Sciences, University of Chicago, US

- Gill Jolly, Director, Merlin Fundraising and Management Consultants Ltd, UK

- Alistair Lomax, Chief Executive, UNIAID, UK

- John Martin, Publishing Manager, Directory of Social Change, UK

- Andrew Watt, Vice President, International Development, Association of Fundraising Professionals, US

- Claire Wood-Hill, Director of Fundraising, Sense, UK.

Participants in Case Study Material Development

- The following UK organizations generously contributed case study material:

ActionAid, Alzheimer's Society, British Heart Foundation, CancerBACKUP, Friends of the Earth, The Healing Foundation,

The Light Box, Lloyd's Market Association, London School of Economics and Political Science, Methodist Homes for the Aged, NSPCC, Richards House Children's Hospice, Royal British Legion, SCOPE , SeeAbility, SPARKs, UNIAID, The Woodland Trust

• The following US organizations generously contributed case study material:

Actors Fund of America, American Museum of Natural History, Asia Society, City Harvest, Crohn's and Colitis Foundation

• The following fundraising professionals kindly provided materials for the case studies:

Mide Akerewusi, Mary Blair, Rachel Case, Joanna Chiffe, Fiona Duncan, Bridget Gardiner, Fidelma Haverty, Richard Hicks, Julie Lang, Alistair Lomax, Tara Mallet, Zoe Macalpine, Jayne McGann, Karl Mitchell, Sean Moriarty, Wally Munro, Giles Pegram, Rachel Perez-Lofty, Maureen Robbins, Ursula Schonbeck-Ceola, Marilyn Scott, Simon Sperryn, Cassie Thompson, Allison Turner, Fiona Turner, Mark Watson, Lynn Weinburg

The Fundraising series

Charity fundraisers change the world by raising the money needed to fund the tremendous good work that charities across the UK carry out day to day. Fundraising moves with the times and is constantly evolving. The economy, political landscape and trends in the way that people exchange information and communicate with each other all impact on the way in which charities ask for, and raise money. This makes the profession particularly dynamic and interesting. In order for fundraisers to be effective, it is vital that they are ahead of the game. Successful fundraisers identify future trends, anticipate demand and keep up with the latest techniques so that they can plan and develop appropriate strategies.

The Institute of Fundraising (IoF) and Directory of Social Change (DSC) fundraising series seeks to address the full range of fundraising activity and techniques in one series. Each successive volume seeks to address one key element in the spectrum of fundraising techniques. As fundraising techniques evolve and develop, new titles in the series are added to and old ones revised. The titles are intended as texts that encourage and debate fundraising within a professional framework – written and used by academics and practitioners alike. Each title seeks to explore the fundraising activity within its historical, ethical and theoretical context, relate it to current fundraising practice as well as guide future strategy.

The IoF is well placed to assist in the development and production of this series; without the support, assistance and expertise of its members and their colleagues, the series would not be possible. I thank all those who have contributed and continue to contribute to the most comprehensive fundraising series available today.

Louise Richards
Director of Policy and Campaigns
Institute of Fundraising

Dedication

We dedicate this book to our husbands Richard Holman and Nick Sainsbury whose unwavering encouragement and support continues to be our inspiration.

About the authors

Margaret M Holman has over 30 years of professional fundraising experience and is president of her own fundraising consultancy in New York City, Holman Consulting.

Email: mholman@holmanconsulting.com

Lucy Sargent has worked in fundraising for 16 years both in the UK and internationally. She has specialised in major donor fundraising for over eight years after developing an interest in this area whilst living and working in New York City. She has worked for a variety of causes and for both large and small charities. Lucy is currently Head of Major Gifts at Marie Curie Cancer Care.

Email: lucy.sargent@btinternet.com

Foreword

Once upon a time, less than two decades ago, not a single trade publication existed for fundraising, books and guides were scarce and those that did exist tended to focus on the type of fundraising done in the community aimed at collecting people's loose change.

This guide by the Institute of Fundraising and the Directory of Social Change concentrates on major gift fundraising and fills a considerable gap. It is the guide I should have liked to have used when I started to try to raise support for my first charity. Lots of people were charming and helpful. But success only came when I had learnt to fundraise from potential donors in an organised and strategic way.

Since then, I've learnt to understand that successful fundraising is reciprocal and that, as Lynn Truss suggests in her recent book on manners, for every good deed there's a proportionate acknowledgment which precisely repays the giver – the aim being for no one to emerge in the red. Fundraising is but a part of the ongoing relationship with a charity's stakeholders.

Relationships are at the core of any campaign, and – just as in life – are made *over time* through tests of trust. One may want to hurry the process up, but it is not advisable as a success tactic. So there are no shortcuts to raising major gifts. Plain and simple: it's very hard work. It takes great chunks of time and bigger chunks of money to raise funds in a sophisticated and thoughtful manner.

I believe that fundraising should always be professional and never fall below an acceptable level. In line with my computing background, I also believe that human memories need to be augmented by database software and that we need to accept that gifts via the Internet will continue to increase in both volume and average value.

The guide's advice is grounded in commercial management practice and common sense. It is not glamorous, but it identifies a step-by-step approach to raising large gifts, repeat gifts, and ultimately legacies. It comes complete with practical tips, how to develop a team approach, and numerous success stories.

Fundraisers will find this comprehensive and practical guide useful in framing their own strategies for success.

Dame Stephanie Shirley
Chair, The Shirley Foundation

Introduction

Welcome to *Major Donor Fundraising*, a hands-on guide for fundraisers, trustees and volunteers who are either new to major gift fundraising or who would like to learn more about this specialised fundraising discipline.

This book came about whilst we were planning a presentation in London for a wide variety of charities to address the issues in identifying, researching, cultivating, soliciting, and stewarding individuals who were capable of making large gifts. Because one of us lives and works in the United States and the other in England, we did separate research on the latest statistics and theories to underpin our presentation. We found that very little information is available to British fundraisers, while at the same time an overwhelming amount of major gift programme facts, theories, and best practices is available to American fundraisers.

This book builds upon current best practices in the UK but also looks to the US to share the experiences, theories, and best practices of American major gift fundraising.

We interviewed charities in Britain and five in the US to provide examples of best practices.

Generally, the charities we interviewed fit into one of three models:

Model One: A small organisation with no major donor base and only one or two staff members.

Model Two: A mid-sized organisation with a few major gift donors and some involvement of high-profile individuals or celebrities through special events. These charities may have a fundraising director or the chief executive is the fundraiser.

Model Three: A mid-sized organisation with the classic appeals committee that helps the staff identify, solicit, and steward major donors. These charities have both a chief executive and a fundraising director involved with fundraising.

This book is organised to reflect the eight steps fundraisers use to encourage major gifts. Each chapter is headed by a list of topics covered in it and includes a synopsis of the chapter's important points, as well as a resource section to give you access to further reading or the source material for the chapter's contents.

Whilst we recognise that applying a blanket approach American-style fundraising in the UK (where a different political and cultural climate influences philanthropy) could lead to debate, we advocate that there is much to be learnt from our US colleagues. We think Oscar Wilde said it best: The Americans are identical to the British in all respects except, of course, language.

Despite the challenges of a global recession, philanthropy continues to be important to people in the UK, the top 100 giving £2.5 billion to causes in 2010. Self-made entrepreneurs are choosing charities over their children to benefit from their wealth with the establishment of major foundations, and the government's Big Society aims to foster a new culture of volunteerism and philanthropy. There has never been a better time for your organization to invest in major donor fundraising.

We trust that you will find our book to be a practical guide that will help you organise and implement a successful major gift programme.

| Margaret M. Holman | Lucy Sargent |
| New York, USA | London, UK |

CHAPTER ONE

Identifying Major Gift Donors: What is a Major Gift and who are Major Donors?

Fundraising is the gentle art of teaching the joy of giving.

— Hank Rosso

Henry A 'Hank' Rosso (1917–1999) was a founder of the Center on Philanthropy at Indiana University (Bloomington, Indiana, US) and founding director of the Center's Fund Raising School.

What you'll learn in this chapter

- Pros and cons of major gift fundraising
- The variety of definitions of major gifts
- The characteristics of major donors
- The types of charities and programmes with the most appeal to major donors.

Introduction

Today, more than 202,000 charities are registered in the UK. By comparison, more than 1,014,816 charities operate in the United States. Keep in mind that the US population is nearly five times that of Britain. The ratio of UK to US charities mirrors that of the population, i.e. each country has about the same number of charities per capita, but despite this similarity, UK charities raised £9.9 billion ($15.84 billion) while US charities raised £189.84 billion ($303.75 billion) from individuals in 2009 – over 19 times the amount raised in the UK. Clearly British charities must work hard to achieve the same level of giving.

Competition is great among charities and continues to grow as new charities compete for philanthropists. Conventional wisdom holds that 80% of all charitable gifts came from 20% of an organisation's donors. The new wisdom recognises that at least 90% of all gifts come from 10% of an organisation's donors. Identifying this 10% segment is the challenge for every fundraiser and the focus of this book.

Pros & Cons of Major Gift Fundraising

Before embarking on a major donor fundraising programme, consider some of the advantages and disadvantages.

Advantages

• Identifies your most important people and allows you to look after them according to their wishes

• focuses on major gift donors who are likely to be long-term supporters and therefore advocates for your organisation

• provides an opportunity to secure legacy gifts through relationship-building

• allows major gifts to be used to leverage other gifts

• mobilises other support from within the networks of major donors

• creates board ownership of the work of the organisation when members are involved with the fundraising for the organisation.

Disadvantages

• Ensures failure will result if your organisation isn't ready to undertake major gift fundraising, e.g. case for support is not developed, systems not in place to undertake good customer care

• doesn't offer a short-term solution for cash injections

• requires a resource commitment to the long term: stop/start approaches will damage relationships with donors

• requires the ability to research and compile donor profiles and fundraising plans

• raises the prospect that staff and trustees in your organisation are unlikely to be educated about major gift fundraising

• requires board members to become involved in the fundraising process by making their own gifts and by helping to identify, cultivate, solicit, and steward donors.

What Is a Major Gift?

How does your organisation define 'major gift'? Is it £5,000 or more? £10,000 or more? £50,000 or more? In a study completed by the Institute for Philanthropy (*www.instituteforphilanthropy.org.uk*), the majority of

British charities interviewed indicated that a major gift was considered to be upwards of £5,000, with a mid-level gift in the range of £1,000, and the lowest-level gifts less than £1,000. Not only do these categories vary from charity to charity, but the passage of time typically plays a part in defining a major gift.

In the 1970s, many American charities considered a major gift to be $1,000. Today, depending upon the size of the charity, a major gift is classified as $25,000 or more. During the ensuing three decades, the pound (or the dollar) just doesn't buy as much as it used to, and ten years from now, the value of the pound again may be less – thus inflating the minimum amount to qualify as a major gift. Organisations must be sensitive to the time-value of money, and must also begin to regard major gifts from a new perspective – that of each donor.

If you haven't yet settled on an amount for your major gift level, keep the following in mind as you determine this threshold.

• Look at your current donor base to see how many individuals are at each level. If you have a significant number at the £100 level, a few at £250, and none at £500, you may want to consider setting your major gift level at £500 for the first three to five years. Once you have more than 100 donors each contributing at least £500, it will be time to create a new major gift threshold of £750 or £1,000. It will be important to review this on a regular basis.

• Review your top donor's gift history. If you see that there are several community leaders or opinion makers whose sizes of gifts are clustered together, you may consider setting that amount as your major gift level.

• Involve your board and CEO. This will be vital to the success of your organisation's major donor strategy, so therefore ensure you discuss these levels with them. Make a recommendation for their consideration and have them help you determine the right amount, keeping in mind that whatever amount you choose will set the bar for other prospects for the next several years.

Whatever the amount your organisation designates as the minimum level of a major gift, its real definition is whatever the prospect or donor considers to be a major gift. For the purposes of this book, we define a major gift as a 'personally significant gift'; that is, the sum that the prospect decides fits into his or her personal philanthropic portfolio.

For instance, a donor's major gift to Organisation A might be capped at £100, because this organisation is not high on that donor's priority list. For the same donor, a personally significant gift to Organisation B might be £5,000, because this organisation has been a favourite charity of that donor for many years. It will also vary depending upon the donor's perception of the organisation's size and need. Determining where your organisation is in a major donor prospect's portfolio takes time, effort, and sleuthing.

A Brief History of British Philanthropy

Philanthropy in the UK traces its beginnings to the early 1600s, when laws were established to promote philanthropy to the emerging merchant class and the country's aristocracy and to raise money to be distributed to the 'deserving poor' or to provide work for the 'undeserving poor'. The Poor Law remained in effect until 1948.

In 1793, an act was passed to provide formal recognition to 'friendly societies', groups of people whose resources were combined to create funds to be used in times of sickness or old age, or for burials. This act was the forerunner of building and housing societies, and encouraged ideals of self-help and self-reliance. These societies rose to their highest profile in the nineteenth century, when private charity expanded enormously in response to extreme poverty and housing shortages. Social science studies conducted during the period found that 30% of inhabitants in many major UK cities were living 'in poverty or want'. These studies and the work of pioneering philanthropists such as Octavia Hill, whose work resulted in an influx of affordable rented accommodation for the poor, played a huge and important role in bringing poverty to the attention of government and other philanthropists. Many of the UK's most well-known charities that exist today were established during this time. Among them is the Royal Society for the Prevention of Cruelty to Animals (RSPCA), founded in 1884, and Barnardo's, a children's charity, founded in 1869.

Most important, these efforts laid the foundation for a recognition of the need for government to intervene, and the state moved decisively into the provision of housing, education, and public health. This trend continued, and in the late 1940s the then Labour government claimed responsibility for hospitals. At this time there was a cultural revulsion against charities, which were seen as a mechanism for patronising the less fortunate. A UK public opinion poll conducted in 1948 found that more than 90% of respondents believed that there was no longer a need for charities in this country.

The blurring of the lines of responsibility between charity and the state has helped to define the culture of giving that exists today. Even today, the distinction of responsibility between public and private sources of help remains unclear in the UK. This, coupled with the absence of systems to make donations tax-deductible, has done little to foster the culture of generosity that is seen across the Atlantic in the US.

It is only in the last 10 years that tides have begun to change in the UK. Recent efforts – such as the Giving Campaign, a national awareness campaign aimed at promoting giving; the rise in the number of asset-rich millionaires from 7,000 in 1990 to 242,000 in 2009; and new efforts to establish more favourable tax regimes towards donations – are sowing the seeds for an emerging culture of philanthropy in Britain.

Identifying Major Donor Prospects

Where to start? It doesn't make sense to compile a list of names with the idea that you'll just start at the top, arrange a meeting or a telephone call with each potential donor and ask for money, hoping they will make a generous gift. To make a major gift, a prospect needs to be qualified as such. Every potential contributor begins as a *suspect*, and if your research confirms their capability and propensity to give, they then become a *prospect*.

Information that may provide clues to wealth

- Career positions and titles

- Geographic location/postcode

- Life events: a marriage or remarriage, death, divorce, retirement, etc.

- Hobbies/interests/membership of clubs

- Key comments: 'We have a second home in Majorca.' Or 'I was just appointed to the HSBC board.'

- Comments that there are no apparent heirs: 'We never had children.'

Begin by analysing donors listed in your database, looking for those who have been giving for a long period of time and whose gifts have been increasing over time. Organise them on an Excel spreadsheet to allow you to sort them alphabetically, by gift size, by date of last gift, etc. Add an extra column for comments and begin to answer the following questions.

Questions to consider

- How much linkage exists between this individual and your organisation?
- How often and at what level has the individual given support in the past?
- What is the person's estimated financial worth? Net worth, total estimated assets, annual salary, etc. are all indicators of wealth. (See Chapter Two for suggestions about how to get this information.)
- Do we know their motivations? e.g. previous service user, family history of giving, etc.
- Existing contacts/relationship.
- What other causes, and at what levels, is the individual currently supporting?

Assign a number for both capacity to give and willingness to give on a scale of one to five. Those with a lowest number will be more highly ranked as major gift prospects.

Your table will begin to look like Table 1.1.

Your analysis should include the total amount ever given to your organisation by the individuals: there are sometimes people who regularly (even monthly) give a moderate amount but over a year or two give a substantial amount and therefore might be capable of making a major gift.

Once you have this information in the table, sort it to show at the top the donors who have given the most and at the bottom those who have given the least. Now select the top 10 or 20, depending upon the amount of time you have to work with each donor and the number of donors who are on your list, and begin filling out a prospect research form on each donor. (See Chapter Two for this form.)

'You need to know quite a bit about your donors – who they are. If you're small, you can't do a lot of research, so you need to identify and prioritise your best donors. Start with your warmest, creaming-off your most generous donors.'

– ActionAid

TABLE 1.1 PROSPECT RANKING CHART

Donor name	Date & amount of first gift	Date & amount of last gift	Highest gift & date	Total amount ever given	Gift-giving capacity	Willingness to give	Overall ranking	Comments
Mr and Mrs Smythe	1992 £25	2010 £250	2009 £375	£3,500	4	1	3.5	Knows CEO and 2 board members
John Browne	1995 £10	2009 £1,000	2009 £1,000	£3,010	2	2	2	Prospect for board membership
Mr and Mrs Miller-Jones	1997 £50	2010 £5,000	2010 £5,000	£23,330	1	1.5	2	Needs more contact with our programme staff
Ellen Butler	1999 £75	2009 £250	2009 £250	£4,050	3	3	3	Needs more cultivation

Characteristics of Major Donors

How do you determine whether someone is a major donor prospect? Perhaps we should start with a definition of wealth. Most people would agree with the *Collins Dictionary* definition of wealth as an abundance of money and valuable material possessions. Traditionally, our concept of great wealth is the appearance of it – having a big house, fancy cars, extensive wardrobes, perhaps a sizeable inheritance, and the ability to buy anything one wants – but this may not be the entirely correct way to qualify people as major donor prospects.

Indeed, in their seminal book *The Millionaire Next Door*, authors Thomas J Stanley and William D Danko define the wealthy as those who 'get much more pleasure from owning substantial amounts of appreciable assets than from displaying a high-consumption lifestyle'. For instance, Fiona Duncan of Capability Scotland, a charity that provides a flexible range of services to support disabled people of all ages, said: 'We don't necessarily look for very rich people to consider them a high-value donor. It is more about loyalty and frequency, as well as gift size.'

Her organisation scans its database and looks for connections between the donor and the organisation. Ms Duncan explains:

> 'We spotted a name in our fundraising database and connected the name to one of our service users, a lady who was disabled at birth and experiencing deteriorating health. This lady had recently fallen, so her name surfaced in the organisation, and the fundraising team was familiar with the up-market area where the donors lived. We discovered the donors were this lady's elderly parents. We began to research the family and invited them to a lunch just to chat about their daughter's progress and the work of Capability Scotland in general. After the meeting, we found out that the donor was the chairman of a company, and we knew that the shares of this company were beginning to climb. We decided to wait until the share price went up, keeping a careful watch of the business pages. We then invited the couple out to dinner and, together with our CEO and external affairs director, shared the plans we wanted to initiate in Edinburgh. Afterwards, the CEO followed up with a handwritten note to the couple. They promptly sent a cheque for £180,000 with a note saying they'd been honoured to meet with the CEO!'

This success story illustrates the point: to find among your donor constituency those who are already giving to your organisation, as they are the most likely to be major gift prospects. The most likely among them are the group who are loyal donors – those who have been giving to your organisation over a long period of time. Look to see whether their giving has been increasing or decreasing over time. Remove the names of the donors whose gifts are decreasing (but don't forget about them, as they may be good prospects for legacy gifts). With those names left on the list, begin to do your research to qualify your prospects.

What Other Characteristics are Common to Major Gift Donors?

The 2008–2009 Charities Aid Foundation (CAF) National Council for Voluntary Organisations (NCVO) *UK Giving* report states:

• 58% of women give to charity compared to 49% of men. But on average men tend to give higher amounts than women.

• 61% are in managerial and professional occupations.

• Slightly more of them are older (65+), but they are represented in all age groups.

• A large proportion of high-level donors live and work in the London area. Less than 1% of people living in London are earning 17% of its income.

Despite this latter fact, don't despair if you work outside the capital, as there are plenty of people out there who have the ability to give too!

There is yet another good way to begin to sort out who might be a major donor. As defined in *The Seven Faces of Philanthropy: A New Way to Approach Cultivating Major Donors*, by Russ Allen Prince and Karen Maru File, donors can be broadly broken down into the seven categories they propose:

1. *The Communitarian* The donor wants to make his or her own community better – 26.3%.
2. *The Devout* The donor has a spiritual connection to philanthropy – 20.9%.
3. *The Investor* The donor will only give after careful consideration – just like investing in a for-profit company – 15.3%.
4. *The Socialite* Giving is fun for this type of donor – 10.8%.
5. *The Repayer* The donor wants to do good as a result of what the organisation did for him or her – 10.2%.
6. *The Altruist* The donor makes gifts from the goodness of his or her heart – 9%.
7. *The Dynast* The donor's family has a long history of philanthropy – 8.3%.

What Motivates Major Donors?

1. *The nature of your mission* Clearly it is important for those wishing to begin a major gift programme or those wishing to enhance their programmes to be mindful of their organisation's mission and marketing messages. Be sure you know that your donors understand your mission, and learn what they think of your work before launching a major gift programme. Donor surveys are a useful way of gathering information and can be conducted by mail or telephone.

2. *The reputation and integrity of the charity* Your charity must enjoy a solid reputation that reassures donors with the means to make large gifts that they will be associated with a charity that is widely respected. Demonstrating competence and efficiency are also important to donors and this is often judged by the quality and quantity of direct mail.

3. *The charity spends donor pounds carefully and wisely* An increase in accessible donor information about charities through websites such as *www.intelligentgiving.com* and *www.guidestar.org.uk* is creating greater transparency and offering donors more choice and information about the charities they wish to support. Charities must be more transparent in how donated funds are spent, sharing with all their donors – and most important, their major donors – where the contributed funds were spent and what proportion was spent directly to fulfil the organisation's mission. Many charities opt to list this percentage prominently (e.g. 'Do Good Charity spends 95p of every pound to feed the homeless'.) on their websites, as part of letterhead stationery, in direct-mail appeals, and on staff members' business cards.

4. *The charity is able to demonstrate impact to the donor* Increasingly donors desire to have personal impact and therefore are seeking reassurance that their contribution makes a difference and is not lost by the support of others or government funding.

5. *The charity is effective in its work* Donors have an overwhelming range of choices, and the message that your charity is leading the field in providing its services is important. Don't be shy about listing your accomplishments – donors like to feel they are part of a winning organisation. Success breeds success.

Once you have culled your list of current donors and researched them, met with them, and asked them for bigger gifts, you may be ready to begin looking outside your current donor pool for new prospects. This is where networking plays an important role in a major gift programme's development process. The challenge is to find new donors among those who already have an affinity with the mission of your organisation.

Two studies in the US of why the wealthy make gifts indicate that belief in the mission of the organisation was the most important reason. A study by the Community Foundations of America and HNW Inc., a wealth marketing solutions company with offices in the US in New York, Boston, and San Francisco, found that the second most popular motive was personal experience with or a connection to the organisation, followed by the programme's strategy, financial performance, and having a personal contact at the organisation. The US Trust Charitable Giving Study of the top 1% of the wealthiest Americans listed the responsibility to share their good fortune as their number two reason for giving. Listed third was an aim 'to meet the community's critical needs', followed by helping an organisation that has benefited them or a friend, and finally to set an example for their children.

These studies are echoed by the UK-based Giving Campaign study from 2004 that listed the desire to 'do good' and 'make a difference', followed by an affinity with the organisation, and financial considerations of the donor at the time they are asked for their gift. We consider it significant that none of the studies found that tax considerations factored into the decisions of donors to make major gifts, indicating that a philanthropic desire to do good overrides personal benefits.

Leave No Stone Unturned

There are a wide variety of places to look for major donor prospects who already believe in your mission. Start with the most obvious place: ask for referrals from your board members, volunteers, staff, clients, donors, friends, and suppliers (e.g. medical personnel, companies). Consider hosting several 'friend-raising' events or, after sending out your survey, ask to visit with your donors to uncover new prospects. Rachel Perez-Lofty at the UK's Alzheimer's Society sent a survey to 25 of her donors. Most responded to the survey, and one-third agreed to meet with her. 'We said that we really wanted to get their advice and understand their experiences with the Society', she said. 'I was very flexible with times and dates and felt quite taken aback when so many of them said, ' "Yes, please come and visit." '

Additionally you should contact those who:

- maintain more than one home

- are large landholders

- give to other similar organisations

- are social leaders in your community

- are religiously active (Asian wealth and philanthropy are growing rapidly)

- are known to agents of wealth – solicitors, trust officers, accountants, and insurance agents.

And don't forget to use your CEO's and board chairman's networks. The development team at CancerBACKUP, formerly a UK-wide orgnisation that helps people live with cancer (now merged with Macmillan Cancer Support), says their CEO and chairman have significant networks they use to contact prospects personally. Maureen Robbins, Head of Major Donors & Special Events at CancerBACKUP, said: 'Our approach is very much about working with individuals and their networks. We're finding people who are moving in the same circles.'

Types of Charities with Appeal to Major Donors

The 2010 CAF/NCVO individual giving report shows that donors give most to medical research, followed by hospitals/hospices and children and young people (joint tied for second place) and overseas organisations.

Conclusion

Identifying potential major donors requires that you carefully review your current donor base, keeping an eye out for those who have been giving frequently or over a long period of time or both. Use as many connections and networks as you can find to help expand your suspect pool into a prospect pool.

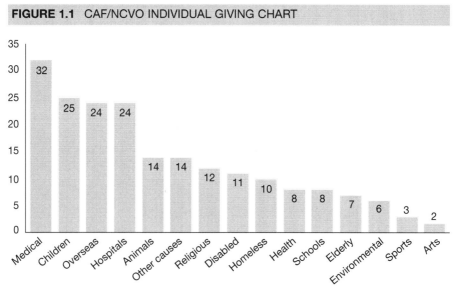

FIGURE 1.1 CAF/NCVO INDIVIDUAL GIVING CHART

Source: NCVO/CAF

References

Affluent Participation in Charitable Giving, US Trust Company, 2000.

A Wealth of Opportunity, The Giving Campaign, 2004.

Bekkers, Rene and Wiepking, Pamela, *Generosity & Philanthropy* A Literature Review, 2008.

Beresford, Philip, *The Sunday Times* Rich List, 2010

Bersi, Robert M, *History, Philosophy, and Standards*. California State University, Long Beach, 2000.

Breeze, Beth, *How donors choose charities*, Centre for Charitable Giving and Philanthropy, University of Kent, 2010

The Heart of the Donor, The Russ Reid Company and Barna Research Group, 1995.

Lannon, Julie, *Managing Major Donors*. The Institute for Philanthropy, 2003.

The Major Gifts Report. December 2003 issue; Special Report: How to Identify and Prioritize Prospects issue; March 2004 issue; Stevenson Inc.

O'Hagan, Brian, *The History of UK Charity*. PNN Online, 2001.

Prince, Russ Alan and File, Karen Maru, *The Seven Faces of Philanthropy*. Jossey-Bass 1994.

Stanley, Thomas J, Ph D and Danko, William D, Ph D, *The Millionaire Next Door: The Surprising Secrets of America's Wealthy*, Longstreet Press.

UK Giving 2004/05, CAF NCVO Report, 2005.

UK Giving 2007/08, CAF NCVO Report 2008.

UK Giving 2009/10, CAF NCVO Report 2010.

What Motivates the Wealthy to Donate to Charity, Community Foundations of America and HNW, Inc., 2003.

CHAPTER TWO

Developing a Strategy for Major Donor Fundraising

What's the use of running if you are not on the right road?

— German proverb

What you'll learn in this chapter

- How to plan to acquire major donor prospects
- How to use Moves Management® with your major donors
- How to set major gift programme goals
- How to retain major donors.

Introduction

Careful planning will help you and your organisation move from the first steps of establishing a major donor programme to the cultivation, eventual solicitation, and continued stewardship of major donors. These plans should address the five areas that will lead you to success:

- the people who are responsible for developing, implementing, and managing this programme

- the budget necessary to ensure the programme's success

- the tools you'll need to help attract and retain major donors

- the timing of the programme

- the benchmarks of success.

> 'One of the challenges for a group starting out in this area is managing the expectations of major donor fundraising – people have an expectation that it will deliver instant big results without having a great deal of understanding about how it's done.'
>
> – Alzheimer's Society

Institute of Fundraising's Code of Practice

A good place to start when developing your major-gift programme is to review the code for Best Practice for Major Donor Fundraising. This code was developed to provide guidance for fundraisers on best practice in raising major gifts.

The code includes information on all of the key elements involved in major gift fundraising including guidance on prospect research, cultivation, solicitation, stewardship, managing gift or donor clubs, and key tax and legal issues. It is published by the Institute of Fundraising and is available free from their website at www.institute-of-fundraising.org.uk

The People Who Make Major Donor Programmes a Success

If you find yourself in what we have defined in the introduction as a Model One organisation (with no known major donor base and only one or two staff), you may think the entire success or failure of the programme depends upon you. But that's not necessarily true, because you should involve many other people in your organisation to help you: the appropriate members of your board, your staff, and perhaps some of those people your organisation helps, such as patients or alumni. Those who are in a Model Two or Three organisation may have more people available to help with the process of major gift fundraising, but they ultimately face the same challenge of implementing a major gift programme.

> 'We're good at utilising relationships with our operations team. Our director is very supportive and understanding about what we do. We work hard to build relationships internally and when staff are invited to support events, they are treated like major donors – it's not just a jolly and they need to be briefed and engaged in the event.'
>
> – ActionAid

One way to expand the number of people to help you with your major donor programme is to create a fundraising committee. The HIV and sexual health charity, Terrence Higgins Trust, has a fundraising committee that is used for networking. The group, which meets for a breakfast meeting three times a year, includes key major donors who work with the staff to increase fundraising. The members of the development group make their own gifts, but generally don't solicit gifts from others; rather, they put forward the names of those who they think may be good fundraising prospects.

During these meetings, take good notes and work with your committee to concentrate on the following items.

- Identify new major gift prospects
- Discuss the next steps for key prospects

- Develop stewardship actions (relationship-building activities) to undertake with individual donors

- Strategise on various funding or naming opportunities for gifts

- Review names of key prospects to be contacted before your next meeting

- Share stories of successful (and not so successful) solicitations

- Celebrate recent successful solicitations.

Others who can be helpful are the members of your board who are willing to cultivate, solicit, and steward donors. Not every board member is cut out to be a fundraiser; in fact, many of them are uncomfortable with the asking process.

> 'A major cultural change has been taking place at Scope as we have made a big effort to educate people in the organisation about major donor fundraising. We've been picking off trustees who are influential and have a good address book and working with them directly.'
>
> – Scope

Some trustees will – after training – become good fundraisers, even great fundraisers. One of the best US fundraisers, E. John Rosenwald, Jr, retired vice chairman at Bear Sterns, has ten rules for successful board fundraisers.

1. Don't ask anyone to do anything you haven't done yourself.
2. Never send a thousand-dollar giver to make a million-dollar ask.
3. Don't give 'til it hurts; give 'til it feels good.
4. Think twice before naming a trustee who can't make a substantial contribution.
5. Never set a campaign goal you can't reach.
6. Never begin the public part of a campaign with less than one-third of the total already raised.
7. Nobody is insulted by being asked for too much.
8. Sell the excellence of the institution. People want to be associated with winners.
9. Be patient. Courting major donors is like catching big fish on light tackle; pull too hard and the line breaks.
10. The sale begins when the customer says no.

Staff members can also be trained to help you with the cultivation and stewardship of donors. Most American colleges and universities include faculty as part of the solicitation team, especially when a prospect or donor's interest is in the faculty member's area of expertise. Asking the staff member to explain what they do, why it's done, and how it's done lends credibility to the programme and often will 'seal the deal' with a major donor prospect. Never ask a staff member to meet with a donor alone; always have at the meeting another person, either a board member who is an experienced fundraiser or the fundraising professional.

The other impressively successful method of involving others in the asking process is to include those who are beneficiaries of your work, such as students or patients in recovery. One of the most successful solicitations we've seen was conducted by an organisation that provided housing for the homeless by rehabilitating old urban hotels with construction crews they trained in a jobs programme. The organisation invited prospective donors to a walk-through just before its new shelter opened. Several of the men and women who had successfully completed the organisation's training had been hired by the construction company, and were to live in the building. They were asked to tell their stories to the prospects that evening. These first-hand poignant presentations by the formerly homeless who were showing their new rooms they'd built themselves was a powerful way to demonstrate to the prospects the effectiveness of the programme and of the contributions the prospects would later make.

Budget

Developing a budget for the major gift programme depends upon which of the models your organisation best fits and the number of activities you plan. For Model One charities, the major gift programme budget may be modest, covering research and cultivation expenses, such as luncheon meetings or an occasional dinner with a major prospect or donor. Model Two and Three charities have additional expenses, including salaries, cultivation events, recognition events, small gifts for major donors, travel, and research resources costs. For instance, one charity we know spent a total of £58,000 plus the salaries of two staff members to raise £900,000. A rule of thumb some people use is that it will cost you at least 10% of what you want to raise.

What to include in your budget

• Research expenses including subscriptions to online and other research tools, depending on what you can afford:

• Computer software (if you are just setting up your programme)

• Salaries and benefits

• Printing

• Travel

- Entertainment (meals with donors and prospects)
- Token gifts and other items in your recognition programme
- Educational opportunities, such as conferences and seminars, and subscriptions.

The Tools for Major Gift Fundraising

What are some of the tools you'll need to begin or expand your major gift programme? There are seven basic tools every major gift fundraiser must have.

1. The most important is the *case for support* – a clear, concise, and compelling rationale for why your prospect should make a large gift. You must take the time to reflect, and then write a short paper that tells your organisation's story – a case statement. Get your major donor prospects to understand and see what you see. This case statement can be one to five pages in length, illustrated with stories and pictures of your organisation's achievements and the people you've helped.

Include true-life stories to open your prospect's heart

- Keep a log of stories about those who have been helped by your organisation. If the story moves you, it's most likely it will move your prospects, too.

- Practice telling these stories. We call this narrative philanthropy. Draw word pictures, filled with emotion.

Important as case statements are – and we know many organisations spend large amounts of money for photographs, and for writing and printing these documents – in our three decades of fundraising experience we have never seen a major donor give *solely* because they received a glossy printed brochure. The case statement is only the first important tool for major gift giving.

There are six key elements of a case for support

1. *A Need* that demands a response
2. *A Solution* that the donor can contribute towards

3. A *Cost* providing the direct link between the need and the solution
4. *Urgency* – giving a real reason not to put off responding
5. *Donor benefits* – what's in it for the donor?
6. *Donor context* – tailoring the offer to the interests of the donor.

When completed, the case for support should pass the 'head and the heart test' – logical, feasible, the right solution at the right price, delivered by the right organisation. It should make the donor want to help and illustrate how your support will make a real difference. However, it does not replace the face-to-face ask.

2. The next important tool is your organisation's *wish list*. This is a multipound-level list that gives prospects an idea of the wide variety of ways to help, as well as a sense of exactly how their money would be used. By asking your operations staff to supply a list of no more than three projects with different funding needs, your list will be easily compiled. Print the list attractively to include with your case statement. Smart major gift officers update the list frequently and may develop several versions of it to tailor to major donor prospects. They will also customise a list for a special major donor prospect to focus on that prospect's personal interests.

3. Access to adequate *research* is a critically important tool for major gift officers. As will be discussed in Chapter Three, a good deal of research can be done on the internet, but don't forget the simple things such as entering your prospect's name on Google or another search engine to check for any articles, and periodically hold prospect-rating sessions to gather information about the prospect from his or her peers who are your key volunteers.

4. The fourth major gift programme tool is *training*. Expecting volunteers and staff to assist in the major gift process without adequate training is asking for failure. Chapter Eight details ways in which you might train your staff and volunteers to help with the major gift programme.

5. Some major donors will ask for a *proposal* that outlines the project and how their major gift will solve a problem or enhance a solution. A good library of proposals covering all of your organisation's programme areas will shorten the process of developing a customised proposal. Remember, the proposal must be clear and understandable and should appear to be easy to read. Allow your reader to digest small portions of information at a time by breaking up the page

into small paragraphs with subheads. Create stories that allow the reader to see how their gift will have an effect on your organisation's ability to provide services.

6. A knowledge of *tax-efficient giving* is a critical negotiation tool. Being prepared with a solid understanding and simple illustrations of tax benefits can influence the decision of a donor and even allow you to negotiate a larger gift for your charity. We recommend you develop your own document for donors outlining how to make a tax-efficient gift to your charity.

Use a proposal as a cultivation tool

Share a two- or three-page proposal with a major gift prospect, explaining that the document is a draft. Ask the prospect to tell you how it should be changed, or ask what's missing or what's most exciting about the proposal. Ask them if this is something that would help them decide to give to you.

Key points to consider about tax-efficient giving include:

● Gift Aid is one of the simplest and most effective ways of giving. Using Gift Aid means that, for every pound given, your organisation will receive an extra 25 pence from the Inland Revenue.

● Donations of shares are exempt from capital gains tax and bequests of shares are exempt from inheritance tax. Recent changes to tax laws make it possible for individual donors who make a gift of shares to deduct the market value of those shares from their taxable income. The same tax benefits apply to gifts of buildings and land.

● Charitable legacies are paid before tax is deducted and therefore offer donors a way of reducing the total amount of inheritance tax due from their estate. In addition, to incentivise the pledging of more legacies to charity, the government has introduced a reduction in the rate of inheritance tax to 36% for estates leaving 10% or more to charity, from April 2012.

● Other methods of tax-efficient giving for donors include payroll giving and setting up a charitable trust.

It is, however, always advisable to encourage your donors to seek independent professional advice when making major decisions relating to personal financial and/or a taxation situation.

For further information see the following:

- Charity Facts: *www.charityfacts.org* includes a useful summary of tax-efficient giving and a handy Gift Aid calculator.

- Charities Aid Foundation: *www.cafonline.org*

- Inland Revenue: *www.hmrc.gov.uk/charities*

7. A well-thought-out *recognition programme* is the final major gift tool. Chapter Seven outlines a wide variety of best practices for donor recognition. Whatever style your organisation chooses, make sure it is liberally applied to your major donors. We believe you can't say 'thank you' often enough. In fact, one organisation we know has consistently lost the support of major donors by infrequently and carelessly recognising its donors. One former major donor said he felt he was a charter member of the organisation's 'donor abuse programme'. Remember that people want to feel valued and appreciated.

Timetable for a Major Gifts Programme

Bridget Gardiner of Richard House Children's Hospice, London's first children's hospice, says: 'There is a story behind each major donor. You don't just get them – you have to grow them in the same way you have to grow other donors.' Major gift fundraising is a patient process and requires time to build a relationship with your prospect. They must know you, know your organisation, feel a connection, and have a sense that their contribution will be used wisely. None of these things happens overnight.

> 'What's important is that you have to make the gift happen, but you can't always control the time frame. It might take 2½ years to meet the person, let alone bring them on board. It highlights the difficulty. You might not even get in the door for a while, then you need to build trust – it all takes time.'
>
> – The Woodland Trust

Nonetheless, major gift programmes can show significant results in three years or less if a plan is created and followed to establish long-term relationships with prospects and donors. Results can be achieved very quickly by upgrading the most promising current donors by asking them to consider making larger gifts each year.

Moves Management®

Charities that implement a Moves Management® system typically find that implementing their major gift programme is 'relatively straightforward'. This system was developed by two Americans, David Dunlop and GT 'Buck' Smith, at Cornell University as a tool to organise and systematise *meaningful* interactions with donors and prospects. It is beginning to be used in the UK but is a relatively new concept.

> 'We use the Moves Management® system and have a prospect list that we go through on a monthly basis, meeting as a team, and from this we develop a fundraising action list for each month. Our Moves Management® system is on Excel and provides a means of keeping up to date with the relationships we have developed from our donors or potential supporters. We have to be strict about keeping this updated, otherwise the information just stays in people's heads.'
>
> – The Healing Foundation

The reason Moves Management® can work is because it helps the major gift officer develop an activity that moves the prospect closer to making a gift. These activities must be carefully planned and put on a schedule to be effective. The activities must be something that has a meaning for the prospect or donor, not just something you list to cross off from time to time. Examples of meaningful moves include:

- Personal meetings
- Visits to your facilities
- Meetings with your staff
- Telephone calls to share information about something new with your programme
- Invitations to special events
- Customised proposals
- Birthday greetings
- Personalised notes (these might include an article about your organisation or a topic of interest to the prospect or donor)
- Personalised greeting cards
- Insider briefings on topics of interest to the prospect or donor.

'You need to be determining – 'what next?' Dinner with a director, lunch with X, sending material, you need to maintain consistent contact. This is about consistent and disciplined behaviour.'

– The London School of Economics

Many fundraising software programmes allow you to track your Moves Management® efforts. To begin your Moves Management® plan, start with an individual cultivation plan, such as the one below.

Individual cultivation plan

Prospect: _____   Date: _____

Primary contact: _____   Primary asker: _____

Anticipated ask amount: £_____

Anticipated cultivation time prior to solicitation: _____

Key information about this prospect:

Those closest to the prospect that can help with the cultivation:

   1.

   2.

   3.

Moves Management Steps

Move_____ Led by_____ By when_____

1. _____

2. _____

3. _____

Updated: [insert date]

Once you have completed a form for each prospect, you should begin to develop your Excel chart that lists the prospects, the activities (or moves), the person who is responsible, the dates by which they are to be accomplished, and the outcome, and leave a blank column for notes. By using the Excel chart, you can easily sort the list by activities, by the dates

TABLE 2.1 SAMPLE PROSPECT ACTION PLAN

Name	Primary contact	Target ask	Activities	Date for completion	Outcome	Notes
Smythe, J	Browne, L	£5,000	Invite to tour facility	April	Called asst & put on his calendar; notified education office of visit	Mr Smythe is very interested in our teaching programme
Jones, M	Browne, L	£1,500	Introduce to CEO	March	Arrange for luncheon with her, Mr Williams, Ms Marx and CEO	Ms Jones is more comfortable in a group. She hasn't come to any event yet, but our board member Ms Marx is a good friend
Miller, S	Holland, R	£5,000	Invite to sit on dinner committee	March	Ask dinner chairman to write letter and follow-up with a call to ask Mr Miller to participate in January dinner event	We think Mr Miller is ready to work on a committee, since he was honoured two years ago
Williams, M	Holland, R	£10,000	Meet to discuss proposal for naming opportunity	January	Arrange mtg to discuss new wing	Is capable of making large gift & is interested in capital expansion
			Prepare proposal	February	Prepare proposal for naming of small conference room	Liked mtg; is open to proposal

by which things are to be accomplished, by the person who is responsible for contact with the donor, by the type of contact, and more (see Table 2.1).

The key to success is to update the information faithfully, review it regularly, and share it with those who will be most helpful to move your prospect to becoming a donor, or to move a current lower-level donor to a higher-level gift.

Setting Major Gift Programme Goals

It is important for you to set goals and objectives for your programme that are achievable, yet are realistically challenging. The old saying 'under-promise and over-deliver' is an important concept to adhere to. Nothing makes for a bigger disappointment for senior management, your trustees or volunteer leadership than failing to meet a fundraising goal by a wide gap. There are some who may think that accurately predicting the amount of money you will be able to raise in the first year of a major gifts programme is impossible – it's not, but it's not easy. A variety of factors need to be taken into consideration, including the number of donors you have, how often they give, how good your case is for giving, how much time you have to devote to major gift fundraising, and how supportive the members of your board can be.

Setting an achievable goal is based on the following factors:

• The number of donors currently in the database who can be identified as major donor prospects.

• The number of giving opportunities that can be clearly defined and presented.

• The level of commitment from the CEO (and if you are a Model One organisation, the level of your commitment to working on a major gifts effort).

A Model One organisation's first-year goals may be to identify research and begin cultivation of its top 20 major gift prospects. During the second year, the Model One organisation should develop a major gift club to recognise these gifts and aim to get 25% of the prospects to make major gifts. (Major gift clubs are covered in Chapter Seven.) During the third year, the up-grading and building process begins with the goal of increasing the number of individuals in the major giving association.

For Models Two and Three, the first year should include closing gifts from 25% of the major donor prospects, as there are more people to help with the process. Generally the goal-setting process should be accelerated for larger organisations with bigger staff and donor bases.

In more developed programmes, it is common for charities to project both a sum of money to be raised and an increase in the number of major donors. Generally, those goals are based on a formula that adds the previous three years of major gift income (subtracting both the largest and smallest gifts) and divides it by three for an average amount raised. This sum is increased, based on the trend the organisation sees when computing the numbers. Other factors are also considered: the inflation rate, the amount of staff and budget available to the programme, whether the organisation is getting ready for a major gift campaign or is already in one, and how much board support is available.

A typical major gift programme projection for a Model One organisation during the second year might look like Table 2.2.

TABLE 2.2 SAMPLE GIFT PROJECTION (MODEL ONE ORGANISATIONS)

Gift size	Number of gifts	Total amount raised	Goal for the year	% of goal reached	Goal for next year	Number of gifts	% increase over previous year's goal
£50,000+	0	£0	£50,000	0%	£50,000	1	0%
£25,000–£40,999	4	£115,000	£100,000	115%	£120,000	5	20%
£10,000–£24,999	9	£95,000	£75,000	126%	£90,000	10	20%
£5,000–£9,999	15	£87,500	£85,000	103%	£90,000	17	6%
Total	28	£297,500	£310,000	96%	£350,000	33	13%

Prospects for each of these giving levels would be listed and ranked with the probability of closing the gift. This gives the major gifts officer a road map for where the money should be coming from throughout the year. As suggested earlier, setting goals will be dependent upon certain aspects that are distinctive to your organisation. For example, if your organisation has not invested in cultivation or donor care to any extent, you may need to spend time drawing your donors closer to your organisation; therefore, your goals may need to reflect this.

As a rule of thumb, you should expect to convert one in seven major donor prospects if you are working with a prospect list that needs significant cultivation.

For Models Two and Three organisations the table might look like this.

TABLE 2.3 SAMPLE GIFT PROJECTION (MODEL TWO ORGANISATIONS)

Gift size	Amount raised in Year 1	Amount raised in Year 2	Amount raised in Year 3	Average amount	Amount projected for Year 4	% projected increase
£50,000+	£50,000	£50,000	£100,000	£66,666	£150,000	50%
£25,000–£49,999	£75,000	£95,000	£100,000	£90,000	£125,000	28%
£10,000–£24,999	£30,000	£45,000	£60,000	£45,000	£75,000	40%
£5,000–£9,999	£25,000	£45,000	£65,000	£45,000	£85,000	47%
Total	**£180,000**	**£235,000**	**£325,000**	**£246,666**	**£435,000**	43%

As well as setting goals for income and expenditures (for the current year and 3-year average), you should also consider setting quarterly and annual measurable objectives for yourself, such as:

• Return on investment

• Number of face-to-face visits you aim to achieve within the year

• Number of new prospects you expect to generate

• Number of face-to-face visits made with the assistance of a trustee or high-level volunteer

• Number of solicitations

• Number of repeat major gifts or major donors increasing their gift.

> 'We manage our programme by objectives. Each regional chapter (depending on where they are with their programme) will need to make X number of face-to-face visits, X number of solicitations and will have a target of achieving X closed gifts.'
>
> – Crohn's and Colitis Foundation of America

Major Gifts Programme Benchmarking

Using the plan outlined above, it is easy to take the temperature of the major gifts programme on a quarterly basis. By simply dividing your year into quarters and assigning the names of your prospects and major gift donors to the appropriate quarter, you can track your progress and see where you may need to do extra cultivation or planning. Depending upon when your major donors like to be asked for their renewed support (or to upgrade their gifts), you can plan fairly accurately when those gifts will be realised. For some organisations, this is at the calendar year-end; however, some organisations base this on when their fiscal year ends.

TABLE 2.4 BENCHMARKING BY QUARTER

First Quarter	Second Quarter
Major Gift Goal: £25,000	*Major Gift Goal: £65,000*
• Upgrade three donors • Hold meetings with 25 donors and prospects • Send first fundraising newsletter • Cultivation event in Sheffield	• Gala dinner • Begin board solicitations • Hold meetings with 25 donors and prospects
Third Quarter	**Fourth Quarter**
Major Gift Goal: £95,000	*Major Gift Goal: £250,000*
• Hold follow-up dinner • Continue board solicitations • Hold meetings with 25 prospects and donors • Send second fundraising newsletter	• Finish board solicitations • Hold meetings with 25 donors and prospects • Close remaining major donor and prospect gifts • Hold holiday party

Working with major donor prospects is another matter – some organisations, such as Terrence Higgins Trust, have developed a fundraising plan that looks something like this:

• Summer gala fundraising pledge dinner for existing supporters and prospects

• Small follow-up dinner for those who cannot attend the gala dinner (perhaps two follow-up dinners annually)

• Face-to-face meetings for supporters and prospects who cannot attend any of the events

• Supporters and prospects receive two newsletters per year

• A non-fundraising thank-you party for supporters and donors at Christmas.

'At ActionAid we have a mixture of cultivation events in our annual plan – one for each type of our major donor audiences. For example, we have:

• Small exclusive pledge dinners: the actress Emma Thompson is one of our Ambassadors and recently hosted a pledge dinner for us.

• Briefing events: our head of emergency team held a briefing event at the head office to update existing Ambassadors. These donors are on the inside track of the organisation.

• Large briefing events: e.g. we held an event at London's Science Museum where prospects, Ambassadors, and other donors were invited.'

– ActionAid

As you can see, it takes time to cultivate and involve prospects to the point that they will make a significant gift that results in moving them into your major donor association.

Retaining Major Donors

Once you have them, how do you keep them? This is an important topic and is covered in detail in Chapter Six. It is vitally important to keep major donors involved in the way in which they want to be included in your organisation. Meaningful involvement with a charity is the top reason major donors stay loyal to organisations. 'We make sure donors feel cared for,' says Cassie Thompson, of the British Heart Association. One of the ways major donors feel cared for is to invite them to spend time with the CEO, and to send them updates by newsletter, e-mail, or personal correspondence. 'If they phone and ask for something,' says Maureen Robbins, formerly of CancerBACKUP 'we'll make sure that it is done quickly, and we keep them in touch with the result.'

The point here is to personalise your contact with each of your major donors. Find out what they want, not what fits into your programme.

According to *Managing Major Donors: How Charities Manage Their Relationships with Donors*, a report from the Institute of Philanthropy and the UK-based Ansbacher Group, the type and frequency of contact with major donors vary: 'Some want regular personal telephone contact, others find too frequent contact unnecessary and can be intrusive. At the very least, donors would like material describing the work of the charity and specifically how the money has been spent and the rewards it has brought, specifically if this is tied to a particular project.'

One of the easiest ways to value the relationship with your major donors is to ask for their opinions. Everyone tends to be flattered to be asked and major donors even more so. Be sure that once you ask for their opinions, you make use of them and follow through by letting them know their opinions affected your project.

> 'We once got a call from a rather disgruntled donor to ask why, for our Gala Dinner, we were returning to a venue where the previous year the food, in his opinion, had not been up to scratch. I apologised profusely and told him we had been unaware of any complaints. It worried me. He was a long-time supporter and someone we should have been developing and not alienating. A month later, it was time for the food tasting. I asked him to join me. He was delighted. He's now one of our key big givers. It's a good example of turning a complaint into a positive experience and how to make the experience personal.'
> – Terrence Higgins Trust

It is important to be sure that not every contact with a donor is to ask for money. Remember, you are trying to build a relationship with your donor that will last over time, so they should be treated as a valued friend. Alison Goodman, of Terrence Higgins Trust, says some of her donors have become good friends: 'I've been invited to their parties. I go to get to know the donors. It's so crucial to build relationships with your supporters.'

References

Affluent Participation in Charitable Giving, US Trust Company, 2000.
Malthy, Butch, Touchpoint Solutions, *The Major Gifts Report*, 2004.
Managing Major Donors: How Charities Manage Their Relationships with Major Donors, The Institute for Philanthropy and Ansbacher, 2003.
The *Major Gifts Report, 2004*, Stevenson Inc., 2004.
McKenzie, Tom and Pharaoh, Cathy, *CGAP Briefing Note*; Thinking through the effect of changes in income-tax relief on giving, 2009.
'When "Rosie Asks"', New York's Elite Can't Say No,' *New York Times*, November 20, 2000.

CHAPTER THREE

Research: How to Find Major Donors

What you'll learn in this chapter

- How to identify and build a list of potential major donors
- How to research and build profiles on individuals
- How to qualify and rank your prospects
- Available online and published research resources.

Introduction

How do you start with a blank piece of paper and build a major gift programme? Many fundraisers initially think that they do not have any potential wealthy donors connected to their organisation, but a little research can uncover huge potential.

Start with what you know. As 80–90% of your group's annual voluntary income is likely to come from 10% of your supporters, you should start with your inner circle – those closest to your organisation. This will include those who already give to your charity, and should involve your chair, trustees, chief executive, senior staff and key volunteers.

Then identify those who might give to your organisation, such as people who have donated to a cause that is similar to yours, those who live near one of your projects, those with moderate wealth, and those with whom you have a contact through a trustee, volunteer or staff member. Remember too the potential for existing donors to introduce like-minded people to your organisation. You will quickly develop a long list of people, and you will need to qualify your list through research.

The practice of prospect research is specialist in its own right. Many organisations with an established major donor programme will have their own in-house staff dedicated to this function. When starting out in major gift fundraising, research is often carried out by the fundraiser or chief executive, particularly in Model One organisations. For those interested in learning more about prospect research, there are several excellent guides, such as *Find the Funds* by Christopher Carnie and *Prospect Research* by Cecilia Hogan and David Lamb. Here, we aim to give you the tools to enable you to identify and undertake the basic prospect research required to qualify your prospects. The purpose of this research is to gather knowledge so that you can have the right conversations when you meet your prospect. As your programme develops, you may want to commission external research through a prospect researcher or research agency, or recruit a specialist into your organisation to undertake this function, although this option is more expensive and not viable for smaller charities starting out in this area.

Internal sources of prospects

Start with those who are already connected with or giving to your organisation, by undertaking some simple analysis of your database and identifying the following:

- Those who have made single or accumulative gifts that exceed a specific amount (if you are starting out, this might be £1,000 over two years).

- Those who have been giving to your organisation for a long period of time and therefore demonstrate loyalty to it.

- Service users or individuals with a connection to your cause through personal experience.

Then build your list by identifying people who have not given but who are connected to people involved in your organisation and who may give if the person in your inner circle asks them. We call this *network research* (see the section later in this chapter, which addresses network research), and it might include identifying friends, neighbours, and business associates of the following individuals:

- contacts of your chairman and trustees
- volunteers and their contacts
- donors and their contacts
- your chief executive's contacts
- your staff's contacts (including suppliers).

You will need to reassure these individuals that names they provide will be well cared for and that approaches won't be made without their consent.

You may decide to undertake your own research into these networks or ask a group of people closely involved with your organisation to write down names of prospects they know or are acquainted with; this process is called *prospect screening*.

After you have completed your internal research, you may wish to add to your list those individuals who may have an interest in your cause but who have not yet given and who are not known to any of your inner circle. These can be identified through specific research.

● Make a list of causes similar to your own and review each organisation's annual report to build a list of donors who give to similar causes or campaigns.

● List people in the media or known community leaders who may have an affinity with your cause either through proximity or personal experience or because they have given to similar causes.

● Commission a specific prospect research project with a professional researcher. For example, SeeAbility, a national visual impairment charity, wanted to identify individuals with a net worth of greater than £5 million and an interest in disability in North Yorkshire. SeeAbility commissioned a prospect researcher to undertake this external research. Thirty potential prospects were identified, with background information on each one provided.

Once you have completed the steps above, you will have developed a long list of people – too many for you to manage all at once. Depending on available resources, you will need to start working with an appropriate number of prospects. If you are a fundraiser with the primary responsibility for major gift fundraising, you should aim to manage a portfolio of approximately 100–150 names. If you are the chief executive or a fundraiser who juggles other responsibilities, you should initially work with your top 25 prospects. The next step will be to qualify and rank your list so that those who are most likely to give are at the top of your list. By focusing on the top prospects, you will be spending time where it is most likely to pay off, and at the start of a major donor campaign this is crucial in order to give you and your organisation the confidence to continue.

Using a prospect research company or consultant

Professional researchers can complement your research and help you identify prospects who are most likely to make significant gifts. There are three main areas where this type of support can add value to your programme.

1. Electronic screening of your donor database

There are a number of database screening products and companies. The purpose of undertaking a database screening exercise is to identify people whose names may be in your database but who have not yet given significantly and who have the potential to give. They work by electronically comparing your database against databases of high-net-worth individuals to look for a match of names. Companies that build these databases do so over many years. They compile known lists, such as the *Sunday Times* Rich List, and undertake research of high-net-worth individuals who prefer to stay out of the limelight. Most charity databases will include 1% or 2% of high-net-worth individuals, and database screening allows you to find them. Large databases may require more frequent screenings, whereas smaller databases of fewer than 10,000 names may need to be screened only every three or four years. You can expect to receive a list or a detailed report on the names that have been identified, depending on the package you choose to commission.

Companies providing this service include:

- Brakeley Fundraising and Management Consultants: *www.brakeley.com*

- FR&C: *www.frandc.co.uk* A full-service research consultancy.

- Prospecting for Gold: *www.prospectingforgold.co.uk* This is a research service to fundraisers and has a large database of wealthy and influential individuals for screening purposes. It also undertakes profiling for major donor fundraising and capital appeals.

- Factary: *www.factary.com* Factary is a research and knowledge agency for fundraisers and philanthropists, and provides a full research service.

- Wealth Engine: A product developed for the US market and now available in the UK, this provides information on more than one million people in the UK. Both Factary and Brakeley provide this data mining and screening service, comparing the names in your database against a database of known UK personal wealth.

- A number of smaller outfits also exist, such as Milestone Research and ResearchPlus, that provide fundraising research services for the not-for-profit sector.

- Many of these companies will provide an initial free screening of your database to give you an indication of the number of matches (but not the individual names) between their database and your own. This will enable you to determine whether it will be worthwhile for you to allocate funds to commission the service. For an indication of costs, see Table 3.1.

> 'We have a database of 160,000 people which we recently screened and found 2,238 people with a capacity to give at the major donor level. It's a bit overwhelming to have so many names to work with. We mailed them an invite to a House of Commons event and had an overwhelming response – almost 700 people! Everyone received a pack and a pledge card at the reception. The hard work will be afterwards when we do the follow-up. It's incredibly important to download conversations from staff after the event.

Many organisations protest that they don't have any major donors, that they don't know any rich people. We believe and know from experience that every organisation that receives donations from individuals has potential major donors.'

– ActionAid

2. In-depth research into a smaller list of names

Prospect researchers can provide in-depth analysis of a small list of prospects for which you pay per name. Information can include details on spouse, children, education, employment, career history, investments, wealth estimate, interest in or links to other causes, and networks, as well as other criteria that you can specify. This type of research can be useful to conduct on your key prospects and leadership, for example identifying networks of people known by your chairman.

The following sample profile illustrates the types of information you can expect to see when you commission a prospect research on an individual.

FIGURE 3.1 SAMPLE STANDARD PROFILE

	DATABASE INFORMATION
NAME	Doe: Mr Joe (John) Doe, OBE
ADDRESS	100, Fortnum Row London SW1 1XX
UNIQUE REFERENCE NO.	XXXX
PROSPECT NAME	Doe: Sir Joe (John) Doe, CBE
HOME ADDRESS	1 Fortnum Mews London SW1 1MM
BUSINESS ADDRESS	Doe Investments plc 100 Mayfair Place London W1 1XX
TELEPHONE	(020) 0000 000
DATE OF BIRTH	1st January 1945
KEY DIRECTORSHIPS	Doe Investments plc – founder and chairman JD plc – non-executive director

Previously: Multinational Bank plc – founder, chairman & president Innovus Ltd - non-executive director |
GRANT MAKING TRUSTEESHIPS	The John Doe Foundation – settlor & trustee Disabled Children's Sports Foundation – vice president
PHILANTHROPIC INTERESTS	Mayfair Festival of Performing Arts – joint chairman The Theatre Council – chairman
WEALTH ESTIMATE	The wealth of John Doe and his family is estimated in the press at £400 million based on the value of his company, Doe Investments plc and the sale of Multinational Bank. He holds shares in JD plc with a current value of £500,000.(Name of Paper, date)
LIVERY & CLUB MEMBERSHIPS	Liveryman, The Musicians' Livery Company Garrick Hampstead Golf Club
LEISURE INTERESTS	Theatre, opera, golf, horse racing, horse breeding
RECENT NEWS	Doe was involved with US private equity group, Capital Venture Plc in a rescue package for the troubled computer software company Softouch. (Name of paper, date)

Sample Profile Pack, The Factory Ltd, 2004   5

3. Undertaking specific research projects

Professional researchers can also work to a specific brief, unique to your organisation; for example, identifying people who have previously made gifts of £25,000 or more to the arts in Scotland.

Do your research before using a freelance researcher or research consultancy, seek references from others, and ask for a free trial or to see samples of research reports. Consider undertaking a detailed comparison between two agencies such as the one shown below. Avoid disappointment all round by reading and approving a detailed brief for the research project. Before commissioning database screening, request a breakdown of the sources and quantities of data used to screen against. Identify the data and format you can expect to see returned to you and how you will integrate this information into your database.

TABLE 3.1 SAMPLE COMPARISON OF ELECTRIC SCREENING SERVICES BETWEEN TWO RESEARCH AGENCIES

Criteria	Research Company Y	Research Company X
Number of names screened against	130,000	82,000
Sources of data	<ul><li>Newspaper Rich lists</li><li>Senior Directors from plcs and private companies</li><li>Key trustees of major trusts</li><li>People who have an entry in Debrett's/*Who's Who*</li><li>Shareholder registers</li><li>Celebrity magazines</li><li>Websites/online archives</li></ul>	<ul><li>UK millionaires</li><li>Directors of UK plcs and private companies</li><li>Trustees of grant-making trusts</li><li>Newspaper Rich lists</li><li>X research companies own database of wealthy individuals</li><li>People who have an entry in Debrett's/*Who's Who*</li><li>Plus others</li></ul>
Name and ID only	£2.50 + VAT per name	Not available
Name, ID and wealth band/value	£5 + VAT per name (provides indication of wealth level)	£4 + VAT per name, (provides indication of donor level, e.g. high, mid, low value, plus Research Guide which provides summary of findings)

Criteria	Research Company Y	Research Company X
Name and descriptive reason	Database Summary Screening Report £10 + VAT per name	Wealth Check Report £10 + VAT per name (minimum £500 + VAT) Doesn't include news/online searches
Profile	£15–30 + VAT per name (depending on how many records, e.g. if 250 it would be £15 + VAT per name)	In-depth profiles start at £100 + VAT per profile (Connections profile also available at £175 + VAT)
Initial electronic screening report Cost for initial screening	Free – determines rough estimate of numbers and costs Free	Free – determines rough estimate of numbers and costs Free
Cost for name, ID and donor wealth indication for 200 records (approx. 1% of database)	£1,000 + VAT	£800 + VAT
Screening timeline	5–10 working days	10–15 working days

Qualifying your Prospect List

When determining the potential value of your prospect to your organisation, you should consider three things we call CCI.

These are the individual's:

- *connection* to the organisation or someone involved in the organisation
- financial *capacity* to contribute a major gift
- level of *interest* in your cause.

Connection

Having a connection enables an opportunity for a relationship. As long as someone is willing to introduce you, you've got a connection. A prospect may be wealthy and have an interest in your cause but have no relationship with you. Others may have attended an event or had some low-level connection with your organisation. Without a connection, it will be much more difficult to reach your prospect. A connection may be business-oriented, such as a fellow board member or colleague, or it may be personal, such as a neighbour, friend, or family.

Don't assume that you need an immediate connection. It could be that the person you want to connect with is a friend of a friend and therefore it may just require more extensive planning to reach them.

Capacity

When determining capacity to give, look for signs of wealth, such as an expensive home, a second home, or a high-paying job. Ideally, you are trying to identify people with liquid assets, especially those who have just come into money and may be looking for ways to spend it.

Capacity to give is also based on personal circumstances and life-stage. If the potential prospect has children at home or in university, you are unlikely to attain a big gift. However, if he or she is self-sufficient or has no children, wealth is more likely.

How do you calculate someone's net worth? Net worth is the total sum of the prospect's assets minus their liabilities. A number of formulae can be used to determine net wealth; however, this is as much an art as a science, and we caution against over-reliance on this type of calculation. Intuition and careful listening are arguably more important in making a sound judgment.

Formulae for calculating capacity to give:

- Giving ability is 1–5% of a prospect's net worth (depending on the level of interest you think the prospect has).

- Multiply the prospect's age by total income (salary, dividends, etc.) and divide by 10.

- If you are considering prior giving history as the basis for a gift, this could be between two and four times the amount of the annual gift multiplied by five (over five years); e.g. previous gift of £5,000, could ask for a donation ranging from £50,000 to £200,000 (over five years).

Interest

This is hard to gauge, but some indicators might include previous gift history, frequency of interaction, attendance at an event, or previous support of a similar cause, as well as having a member of the family with a connection to your cause.

Evaluating the data you find when looking at connections, capacity, and interest requires an element of best judgement and intuition. This is necessary, because none of your sources will be 100% accurate, and in many cases, you will be working with incomplete information. Be aware that some information may be outdated, particularly when assessing property values. When rating capacity to give, potential wealth is only an indicator in general. How much the prospect will give is up to you and your cultivation efforts.

Peer Screening

Talking to your inner circle of volunteers, trustees, and chairman is one of the best ways of gathering information about your prospects and adding new ones to your list. The advantage of these screenings is that they often provide subjective information. However, it is almost never productive to ask, 'Do you have any contacts we could have?' or 'Do you know anyone rich?' This is sure to elicit a negative response. Instead, you need to facilitate this process. Start by providing the A–Z list of prospects you developed through the stages listed above. This list might include prominent people in the community, existing supporters who you are trying to reach, or business people you have identified. It is much easier to respond to a list that will prompt other names than to stare at a blank sheet of paper.

The process can be done in a group setting or one-to-one. A group setting has the advantage of creating a healthy sense of competition about who knows who and should encourage those who may feel less forthcoming about their network. Alternatively, you may wish to ask a few well connected donors or volunteers to meet with you privately. This can be time-consuming but can elicit valuable information. Often a two-stage process works best – initially get a group together and use the competition element as well as people helping each other with the 'brainstorm' process, then follow up on a one-to-one basis for further information when you can ascertain how good the contact is and gather additional information that people may not have felt able to share in the group environment.

'When developing a prospect, look for matches between your needs and the areas of interest of the prospect. Look for linkages with your leadership.

When working with trustees or senior staff to review prospects, be honest. It's OK to ask for help. Be well-prepared. Go with your list of people, make sure that names are spelt properly and that documents are well laid out. Be specific. Say "Can you help me with this . . . by doing X".'

– CancerBACKUP

November 2005   1 of 1

Steering Group Peer Review

KEY (for conducting peer review)

> **How well do you know them?**
>
> 1 = Do not know
>
> 2 = Know slightly (eg. to say hello to at social gathering)
>
> 3 = Know quite well (eg. on the same board, member of the same club, but do not know very well)
>
> 4 = Know well (eg. know well socially or business associates)
>
> 5 = Know very well (eg. Close friends/ contacts)
>
> **Potential:**
>
> Please tick the relevant column to indicate if you think the individual has potential as:
>
> - **Appeal Chair**
> - **Committee Member**
> - **Prospect (Donor)**

NOTES:

- Please note that the research was conducted in Summer & Autumn 2005 & may since have been subject to change.

- **Database Screening Methodology (WealthScan)**
  Cascaid Consulting conducted a screening of CancerBACUP's database in 2004 to identify individuals capable of making significant/ major donations. The screening involved matching names and postcodes against WealthScan, a wealth assessment screening tool which, based on analysing a number of key indicators, identifies potential donors and assesses prospects ability to give, based on wealth.

  Although shareholdings and land/property are analysed, they do not form the basis of the assessment, which focuses on disposable income and giving habits. Estimates are conservative and, given the inherent difficulties of accurately estimating wealth, not necessarily completely accurate.

- **WealthScan Bands:**

  Band A = Capacity to give over £1m
  Band B = Capacity to give over £500,000
  Band C = Capacity to give over £100,000

- **Incomplete Data**

  In some cases, although an individual appears on our database, their record has little information pertaining to contact history and/or financial history with CancerBACUP and we have been unable to ascertain the extent or nature of their involvement.

40

During this process, you will want to identify:

• connections: for example, how well a member of your leadership knows the prospect

• capacity: for example, any background information relating to their personal circumstances and an indication of potential gift size

• interest: for example, their preferences or interest in any particular area of your work.

Planning considerations

• Database and peer screening are part of the preparation and planning required to undertake major gift fundraising. You need to incorporate these activities into your timetable, as they will need to take place before you will be in a position to ask for a major gift.

• You will need a budget to purchase external services, such as electronic screening and any in-depth research that you may want to conduct on a few key people.

• Staff time will be required to manage the process. Specific jobs will include analysing the database screening, organising a peer screening session, rating and ranking prospects, and undertaking further in-depth analysis of key prospects.

Prospect Research

In addition to peer screenings, you may also wish to undertake some specific prospect research on your emerging key prospects. The internet has a wealth of information on individuals, all of it public and most of it free. Some services can be accessed at a small price, and many offer free trial subscriptions, allowing you to test the service to see whether it will work for you. At the end of this chapter, you will find a list of useful research resources and information websites.

There are numerous reasons to undertake prospect research. You might be seeking to identify a connection with your prospect to help you with an introduction. For example, if your prospect – let's call him Alan Wilcox – is a known trustee of the Good Work Foundation, look at the names of its other trustees. You might also look for employment-related networks, for example if Alan works for a leading investment bank see who else works there on a similar level. You could then look at who else works for other investment banks at that level. You might also learn where

Alan previously worked and look for people who worked there at the same time.

You might also look up Alan's profile on Debrett's (if you subscribe to or can access this service via your library) which publishes data on individuals of significance in British society. If he went to Cambridge in the early 1960s, you could then run a search on Debrett's online service to see who else went to Cambridge during that time to try to pinpoint people he might know. You might try a postcode search on your database to find out if you have a donor who lives nearby and who might know Alan. Try running searches of Alan's name on Google to identify social reports or interviews in which he may have talked about his personal interests or social life. Also think about members of Alan's family – parents, spouse, children (who may be grown up and have good connections themselves or provide a route in to Alan).

At other times, you might be seeking to glean as much information about the individual as possible so that you are prepared to engage him or her with the best chance of success. This might range from honing your understanding of personal interests so that you can match them to an appropriate project, or you may want to review their directorships to identify funding opportunities through his or her network.

Who's Who lists individuals' interests which can provide a useful way in – one fundraiser we know brought onboard a major donor who later became a president of a conservation charity by discovering one of his listed interests: bird watching.

Collating the information

The information that you gather from these efforts should be added to your database or master list, normally in note format. However, for your top 30–40% of prospects, you should develop in-depth profiles and create an individual file for each prospect. This allows you to collect information – including news articles or other information that may help you with the cultivation of the prospect – and keep it in one place. Prospect worksheets such as the template shown opposite can be created in a Word document, linked to the database record, or stored on the database record itself.

Five things to know about each of your prospects

- What will motivate them to give?
- What are their personal and professional priorities and circumstances?
- Which other charities do they support?
- What do they like or dislike about your organisation's work?
- Whose phone call would they most likely return?

FIGURE 3.3 SAMPLE INDIVIDUAL PROFILE FORM

INDIVIDUAL PROFILE

Full Name:	
Address:	
Phone:	
Fax:	
Email:	
Date of Birth:	
Family:	
Education:	

Career Précis:	
Current Directorships:	
Previous Directorships:	

Estimated Worth	
Trusteeships	
Philanthropic Activities	
Links to Client	

Recreations	
Clubs	
Other Information	

This profile was created for (client) by Saints Information (www.saintsinformation.co.nz) on 16/11/05. Note that the information has been compiled from a variety of published sources – many of which date very quickly

Prioritise Your Prospects

The next step is to use the information you have gleaned to prioritise or rank your prospects. Moves Management® is a two-part system that we described in Chapter Two. The first part involves ranking your prospects, and the second part maps cultivation and solicitation activities. This two-part system enables you to cluster your prospects so that you can identify and work hardest on those with the greatest potential, as well as track moves that draw the prospect closer to your organisation.

Ranking systems enable you to apply a number or a code to prospects so that you can categorise them systematically. You can devise a simple system for your organisation or use a more complex formula. Ratings are an amalgamation of data from the many sources that we have identified above, including prospect screening, database screening, or your own prospect research. Furthermore, a ranking system demonstrates how much information you have (or might not have) about your donors and prospects. If you aren't able to judge someone's interest or capacity to give, you won't be in a position to ask them for a donation. Once you have established a system, you need to ensure consistency of application.

Ranking can be established by assigning a code to *propensity* to give (or interest in giving) and *capacity* to give, as indicated in the following table. Propensity is arguably the more important of the two: your prospect may have lots of money, but if he or she has no predilection to give, you are unlikely to be successful. Capacity to give is best identified through external sources, while propensity to give is best identified internally.

TABLE 3.2 PROSPECT RANKING CODES

Capacity to give	Code	Propensity to give	Code
£50,000+	1	Very active, enthusiastic, and ready to give at the required level	1
£50,00–£25,001	2		
£25,000–£10,001	3	Active and interested, and requires minimal cultivation	2
£10,000–£5,000	4	Moderately interested, requires some cultivation	3
Unqualified/unknown	N	Minimal or no interest, requires extensive cultivation	4
		Unqualified or unknown	N

By adding the two numbers, capacity and propensity, you can determine a prospect's overall priority rating. Those with the highest scores will require the most cultivation. The best strategy is to reserve the bulk of the effort for prospects with major gift potential who are already slightly involved.

● 2–3: These are your best prospects. They are the most committed and have the greatest potential to give.

● 4–6: These prospects are the second most important and need the focus of your cultivation activities.

● 6–8: After you have addressed the categories above, turn to this group. Some of these may not be worth pursuing now, but you don't want these prospects to disappear from your list altogether.

Your next steps will include:

● setting up a cultivation plan and timeline for your best prospects

● assigning top-rated prospects to appropriate staff or volunteers for solicitation

● inviting new prospects to group events, such as dinners or galas to introduce them to your work.

Table 3.3 illustrates how you can begin to use the Moves Management system to prioritise and manage your prospects.

Other methods used for ranking include assigning a code for different life-stages to indicate the level of available disposable income and therefore the ability to make a major gift. For example, you might use marketing classification systems that relate to life-stage and assigning a code as follows:

● 3 Bachelor stage, double-income no kids (DINKs): wealth is likely but individual is still young and building career

● 2 Full nest (meaning more than one child): usually at the peak of their careers, unlikely to be disposing of income at significant levels

● 1 Empty-nesters: children are grown and self-sufficient, therefore wealth is likely to be more certain.

Alternative coding methods include assigning a letter for propensity, e.g. A – enthusiastic/high involvement, B – some involvement/enthusiasm, C – little or no involvement, and Z – unknown interest, instead of two numerical codes. This allows you to concentrate on prospects ranked 'A'.

TABLE 3.3 SAMPLE MOVES MANAGEMENT® PROSPECT GRID

Moves Management Prospect Grid
Example

#	Prospect	Interest	Capacity	Sum	Potential	Target Gift	Lead Staff	primary volunteer	Interest	Action #1 January	Action #2 February	Action #3 March	Action #4 April
1	Sylvia Turner	1	1	2	£1,000,000	£200,000	CEO	Lionel	Inclusion		Written CEO invite	CEO Lunch/Phone Follow-up	Phone follow-up
2	James Morgan	1	1	2	£1,000,000	£100,000	David	Alison	General support		Written CEO invite	CEO Lunch/Phone Follow-up	
3	John McLaughlin	2	1	3	£200,000	£200,000	Jenny	Lionel	Birmingham focus	Arrange Birmingham project visit	Call to invite to lunch	CEO Lunch/Phone Follow-up	
4	Humphrey Case	1	2	3	£150,000	£50,000	Jenny	Michael	Children's services	Arrange Tadley Project visit	Written CEO invite	CEO Lunch/Phone Follow-up	Phone follow-up
5	Frank Trivett	1	2	3	£1,000,000	£100,000	Alister	David	Activity centres	Arrange Tadley Project visit	Written CEO invite	CEO Lunch/Phone Follow-up	Phone follow-up
6	Anita McIntyre	1	2	3	£500,000	£25,000	CEO	Michael	unknown		Written CEO invite	CEO Lunch/Phone Follow-up	
7	Dudley Havering-Smith	2	2	4	£25,000	£5,000	Jenny	Michael	General support		Written CEO invite	CEO Lunch/Phone Follow-up	
8	Richard Hurst	2	2	4	£50,000	£10,000	Jenny	Michael	General support		Written CEO invite	CEO Lunch/Phone Follow-up	
9	Alison O'Connell	2	2	4	£5,000	£5,000	Jenny	Michael	Helpline		Written CEO invite	CEO Lunch/Phone Follow-up	
10	William Brown	2	2	4	£100,000	£50,000	Jenny	Michael	Helpline		Written CEO invite	CEO Lunch/Phone Follow-up	
11	Alistair Grant	1	3	4	£500,000	£25,000	Jenny	David	eye care project		Written CEO invite	CEO Lunch/Phone Follow-up	
12	Stephen Jones	1	4	5	£10,000	£10,000	David	Alison	Children's services	Meet with Project Dir.	Call to invite to lunch	CEO Lunch/Phone Follow-up	Phone follow-up
13	David Hester	3	1	4	£100,000	£100,000	Jenny	David	General support		Call to invite to lunch	CEO Lunch/Phone Follow-up	Phone follow-up
14	Jane Smith	3	2	5	£100,000	£25,000	Alister	David	unknown		Written CEO invite	CEO Lunch/Phone Follow-up	
15	James Delaware	3	2	5	£20,000	£10,000	CEO	Michael	Inclusion		Written CEO invite	CEO Lunch/Phone Follow-up	Phone follow-up
16	Oliver Johnson	2	3	5	£50,000	£25,000	David	David	General support		Written CEO invite	CEO Lunch/Phone Follow-up	Phone follow-up
17	Michael Spencer	2	3	5	£100,000	£50,000	Alister	Lionel	General support		Written CEO invite	CEO Lunch/Phone Follow-up	Phone follow-up
18	Penny Juniper	1	4	5	£25,000	£5,000	Alister	Lionel	unknown		Written CEO invite	CEO Lunch/Phone Follow-up	
19	Karen Davis	4	2	6	£50,000	£25,000	Jenny	Lionel	Children's services	Lunch with Project Dir.	Call to invite to lunch	CEO Lunch/Phone Follow-up	
20	Fred Winton	3	3	6	£10,000	£10,000	Alister	David	General support		Call to invite to lunch	CEO Lunch/Phone Follow-up	Visit outreach coordinator?
21	David Matthews	4	2	6	£100,000	£25,000	David	Lionel	General support		Written CEO invite	CEO Lunch/Phone Follow-up	Phone follow-up
22	Elizabeth Williams	3	3	6	£75,000	£25,000	Jenny	Michael	General support		Written CEO invite	CEO Lunch/Phone Follow-up	Phone follow-up
23	Simon Roberts	3	4	7	£10,000	£10,000	CEO	Alison	General support		Written CEO invite	CEO Lunch/Phone Follow-up	Phone follow-up
24	Robin Black	3	4	7	£25,000	£5,000	Alister	David	Children's services	Birthday card, 1/28	Written CEO invite	CEO Lunch/Phone Follow-up	
25	Edward Coombs	4	4	8	£250,000	£20,000	Jenny	David	Helpline		Call to invite to lunch	CEO Lunch/Phone Follow-up	Share helpline strategy
					£6,320,000	£1,620,000							

When developing and implementing a system, be aware that you need to balance activities between analysis and cultivation. Try not to get tied up in the coding and analysis stage.

'We could always be doing more face-to-face approaches, but we have to spend time coding the database to allow us to segment the donors in the most effective way possible. It's something that needs to be done – but sometimes these sorts of activities can distract you from talking to donors. It can seem never-ending – the more sorting out of systems you do, the more you realise how much more you need to do.'

– ActionAid

An important point to emphasise here is that many fundraisers and committees spend too long in the 'comfort zone' of researching and cultivating their prospects. It's critical to recognise this fact and be ready to 'move on' to the ask.

Data Protection and Research Ethics

Some organisations have concerns about acquiring personal information about individuals and, in particular, complying with the legislation that governs this in the UK, the Data Protection Act of 1998. Donors have a right under this law to see any information that you store on them.

The Act states eight key principles that must be adhered to in relation to the collection of data on individuals. Data must be:

- fairly and lawfully processed
- processed for limited purposes
- adequate, relevant and not excessive
- accurate
- not kept for longer than is necessary
- processed in line with the data subject's rights
- secure
- not transferred to countries without adequate protection.

In addition, information about individuals must not contain sensitive data.

The Institute of Fundraising has a code of practice that can be downloaded from its website; this draws attention to the areas of the law that apply to fundraising activities.

In addition, the Institute's Special Interest Group for Researchers in Fundraising have developed a set of guidelines regarding compliance with the law. The document aims to address ambiguities within the law specific to the function of prospect research . . . specific to the function of prospect research. A copy of the document entitled A Document of Guidelines in Response to Concerns of Members of the Researchers in Fundraising Special Interest Group Regarding Prospect Research and the Data Protection Act, November 2004 can be downloaded from *www.tinyurl/prospectdata*.

In addition, The Major Donors Code of Fundraising Practice, published by the Institute of Fundraising in 2006 also includes a section on prospect research. This document can be downloaded from the Institute of Fundraising website.

Research Resources

Here is a sampling of the most useful research resources and information web sites to assist you with your research efforts. Many are available free of charge from good libraries. When using research resources, especially via libraries, always check that you are not in breach of the licence conditions. Your prospect research needs will be dictated by your fundraising needs. If you cannot afford the best, you can probably afford something similar, or even access it for free.

Three general resources to look at

1. THINK Resource provides information on over 1,000 resources to find what you want. Please note that it is no longer being updated (and hasn't been for some time) *www.thinkcs.org*

2. The Prospect Research Toolkit provides an excellent guide to a wide range of prospect research resources, and a useful and entertaining blog. *www.fundraisingresearch.info*

3 Public Libraries on the Web to see what resources are available in your local libraries. *http://tinyurl.com/weblibs*

Researching People

• Create a News Alert for each of your top 10 prospects. You will automatically be alerted to any published news about that individual. This might help you be one of the first to congratulate a recent success or provide you with information about business or personal circumstances. Free News Alerts are available from NewsUK (see below) and from search engines such as Google and Yahoo.

• Debrett's *People of Today* is published annually listing 'the leading figures in modern Britain'. It is available as a book, CD and online. The CD allows you to add your own notes and highlight records, then transfer those changes to the following year's CD. *www.debretts.co.uk*. Please note that a fairly recent version of Debrett's *People of Today* is included in KnowUK and Credo Reference (see below).

• *Who's Who* is published annually and contains over 30,000 brief biographies, of 'noteworthy and influential individuals, from all walks of life, worldwide'. It is available as a book and online. *www.ukwhoswho. com.* A fairly recent version of *Who's Who* is included in KnowUK (see below).

• KnowUK is an online database of over 100 reference books including Debrett's *People of Today*, *Who's Who*, *Who's Who in Scotland*, *Who's Who in Northern Ireland* and many others. This is often available free via a local library. *www.knowuk.co.uk*

• Credo Reference (formerly xreferplus) is an online database of over 100 reference books including Debrett's *People of Today*, Debrett's *Peerage & Baronetage*, *Who's Who*, *The Macmillan Dictionary of Women's Biography*, *The Penguin Biographical Dictionary of Women* and many others. This is often available free via a local library. *www.credoreference.com*

• *Who's Who in the City* features biographies of over 15,000 'city executives', with information on professional advisers, and almost 5,000 'major city firms and their regional offices'. *www.wlrstore.com/caritas-data.* Mailing lists based on information in the book are available from Waterlow - *www.wdmlists.co.uk*

• Newsco publish rich lists for a number of UK regions including the Midlands, Wales, Yorkshire the South West and North West of England, and for Wales. Some information is available online, and back issues can be ordered for a small fee. Please note that the archives are no longer searchable for free downloads. *www.newsco.com*

• Archant Magazines also produce regional magazines, some of which include rich lists. Free registration is required to search the archive. If they don't currently produce a rich list for the region you are looking at, ask them if they can do so – you never know! *www.archantlife.co.uk*

Researching Companies

• Companies House Direct lists all public and private companies and limited liability partnerships registered in the UK. Monthly subscriptions are available, and a director search or set of company annual accounts may be downloaded for a small fee.

• Bureau van Dijk produce various company information products – DVD and online. For example, DASH allows you to search for directors and shareholders by home addresses. Other companies produce similar products – Experian's Corporate Researcher *www.experian.co.uk*, ICC *www.icc.co.uk*, and OneSource Business Information *www.onesource.com*

• Hemscott provide some free information online on UK plcs. GURU lists plc companies, their directors with remuneration packages, brief biographies, etc. *www.hemscott.com/guru*

• Northcote provides links to annual reports and other financial results published by listed companies. Northcote often includes annual reports than might be featured on the companies own website. *www.northcote.co.uk*

• Digital Look is a website for people buying and selling shares, but anyone can sign up for free information – company news, directors' share-dealings, free annual reports, etc.

• *The Scotsman* produces email newsletters, and a range of special features e.g. 'dealmakers' business award winners, etc.*www.scotsman.com*

• The Belfast Telegraph lists the Top 100 Companies in Northern Ireland, and publishes a monthly magazine for Northern Ireland. *www.belfasttelegraph.co.uk*

• Newsco (see above) publish lists of the top companies for a number of UK regions including the Midlands, Wales, Yorkshire the South West and North West of England, and for Wales. Some information is available online and back issues can be ordered for a small fee. Please note that the archives are no longer searchable for free downloads. *www.newsco.com*

• Yahoo! Finance includes information on UK plcs, etc: *http://uk.finance.yahoo.com*

• *The Guide to UK Company Giving* lists around 600 companies, detailing their cash donations and other forms of community support. It is available as a book and online. *www.dsc.org.uk*

• *The Hollis Sponsorship & Donations Yearbook* lists over 1,000 of the top companies in the UK which use sponsorship as part of their marketing strategies. *www.hollis-sponsorship.com*

• CommunityMark 'is the UK's only national standard (for business) that publicly recognises excellence in community investment'. *www.bitc.org.uk*

Researching Philanthropy

• The Directory of Social Change produce a range of bookstand online resources *www.dsc.org.uk*

• Caritasdata publish *Who's Who in Charities*, the monthly Charity Funding Report, charityfunding-online, etc. *www.caritasdata.co.uk* *www.charityfunding-online*

• Profunding have a subscription website detailing news and information about new sources of funding. *www.fundinginformation.org*

• The Charity Commission lists charities registered in England and Wales. The website has some charity accounts online. Check Guidestar UK for accounts of smaller charities not shown here. The website also shows other charity interests of trustees, and you can email the Charity Commission for the registration documents of new charities. *www.charity-commission.gov.uk*

• Guidestar UK uses Charity Commission data and also allows you to search by postcodes, as well as keywords, such as surname, etc. it sometimes includes accounts for smaller charities even if they are not listed on the Charity Commission website. *www.guidestar.org.uk*

• The Office of the Scottish Charity Regulator lists charities registered in Scotland. You can also search by postcodes, as well as keywords, such as surname, company name, etc. if you want to ask the correspondent for accounts, etc., be sure to cite the wording on the legal requirements as shown on the page showing each charity summary. *www.oscr.org.uk*

Researching Property

• *www.landregisteronline.gov.uk* Land Register Online provides easy access to details of more than 20 million registered properties in England and Wales. Copies of title plans and registers held in electronic format can be downloaded in PDF format for a small fee.

• There are numerous websites allowing you to search for UK house prices for free. NB see also Zoopla Property Rich List, etc. *www.zoopla.co.uk, www.ourproperty.co.uk, www.houseprices.co.uk and www.nethouseprices.com*

• *www.primelocation.com* is a useful website for accessing details of property from a wide range of estate agents. Where are the properties on sale for over £2 million in Shropshire or Perthshire, etc? Log on and this website will tell you. You can also sign up for alerts, telling you about houses that become available in the future.

• Where are the country estates owned by the wealthiest people in the country? Some of them are listed in these books - *Who Owns Britain and Ireland* (*www.who-owns-britain.com*) and *Who Owns Scotland* (*www.who ownsscotland.org.uk*). Some information is also available on the websites.

• Directory enquiry websites allow you to search for phone numbers. *www.bt.com* *www.192.com* – you can search by postcode as well as name. 192 also sell a number of CDs and DVDs based on the electoral roll, Companies House data and other sources *www.infobel.com/en/uk* – you can search by postcode as well as name. Infobel also sells a range of CDs

Researching wealth

• *The Sunday Times Rich List www.thetimes.co.uk*. Search for details of the top 2,000 wealthy people in the United Kingdom, on the *Sunday Times* Rich Lists.

• *The Sunday Times Rich List 2010* lists the top 1,000 wealthiest people in the United Kingdom and is published each year in April.

• Salary surveys

The annual *Financial Director Salary Survey* and other features are available online. www.financialdirector.co.uk

Researching connections

• *WealthWatch* is a monthly publication produced by Sunrise Publishers Ltd. Each edition contains in-depth detail on the backgrounds, interests, careers and lifestyle of wealthy and /or high profile people. It includes information on their networks and connections. *www.sunrisepublishers.com*

• The Directory of Social Change www.dsc.org.uk produces a wide range of resources on researching grant-making trusts. Their trustfunding website allows you to search by trustee name to identify if your prospect is a trustee of a trust. *www.trustfunding.org*

• *The City of London Directory & Livery Companies Guide* lists members the London Livery Companies. *www.seatrade-global.com*

Researching News

• NewsUK is an online service providing international, national and regional news, currently including 100 newspapers and magazines. This is often available free via a local library. Some libraries use NewsBank, InfoTrac or other services. *www.newsuk.co.uk*

• More comprehensive (and expensive) resources include Lexis Nexis (*www.lexisnexis.co.uk*) and Factiva (*www.factiva.com*).

Other Useful Websites

• This discussion group is open to all researchers fundraising roles in the UK, or anyone researching UK prospects: *http://groups.yahoo.com/group/ prospect-research-uk*

- The Institute of Fundraising's special interest group for trust and statutory fundraising in the UK *http://uk.groups.yahoo.com/group/ trust_fundraising*

- This group aims to provide a forum where major donor fundraisers can share their knowledge, experience, updates on information, and best practice unique to fundraising from major donors. *http://uk.groups.yahoo.com/group/mgsig*

- The Institute of Fundraising's special interest group for Corporate Fundraising in the UK.

http://uk.groups.yahoo.com/group/corporate_fundraising

- Around 90,000+ researchers, at least one of whom will be able to find that missing resource or piece of information at *www.freepint.com/index.html*

- ResearchPlus lists several pages of resources on its website *www.researchplus.co.uk*. See also, Finbar Cullen's PowerPoint presentations on some of the discussion groups listed above, and check out his blog on *www.fundraising.co.uk*

- Factary has a list of resources on its website *www.factary.com*

Institute of Fundraising Special Interest Group: Researchers in Fundraising (RIF).Rif organises conferences, usually in London with guest speakers. Further information can be obtained from the Institute of Fundraising website or by emailing, *researchers@institute-of-fundraising.org.uk*

We gratefully acknowledge the support of Finbar Cullen, ResearchPlus, (www.researchplus.co.uk) who compiled the section on Research Resources above.

References

Stanley & Danko, *The Millionaire Next Door.*
Carnie, C, *Find the Funds*, The Directory of Social Change, 2000.
Hogan, C and Lamb, D, *Prospect Research: A Primer for Growing Nonprofits*, Jones & Bartlett, 2003.
Data Protection Action Group: *A Document of Guidelines in Response to Concerns of Members in Researchers in Fundraising Special Interest Group Regarding Prospect Research and the Data Protection Act*, November 2004 *http://www. institute-of-fundraising.org.uk/documents/RIF_concerns2.pdf*
Data Protection, The Institute of Fundraising's Codes of Fundraising Practice, June 2002.
The Major Donors Code of Fundraising Practice, Institute of Fundraising, 2006

CHAPTER FOUR

Cultivating Major Donors

Mighty oaks from little acorns grow.
— Unknown

What you'll learn in this chapter

- What cultivation is and why it is important
- Planning a cultivation programme for your organisation
- The types of cultivation techniques that are effective.

Introduction

Cultivation is often compared to courting – getting to know your potential major donor with the intention of developing a lasting relationship. As with any form of relationship-building, it flourishes when it is reciprocated. Your donor benefits, and so do you. You learn more about them, gaining more information about their interests and their capacity to give, and in turn, they learn more about you and the work of your organisation. The purpose of cultivation is to deepen significantly the relationship and understanding an individual has of your organisation, programmes, and goals.

Relationship-building cannot be rushed. It requires patience, sincerity, and commitment. Once you have identified your major gift prospect, it may take you six months to secure your first meeting. This first getting-to-know-you meeting rarely results in a significant gift. The time required to deepen the relationship before your new friend will be confident and committed to saying yes at a more significant level will vary. For this reason, of the four key phases involved in major gift fundraising – prospecting, cultivation, solicitation, and stewardship – cultivation takes the longest. You should allow anywhere from six to thirty-two months for a major gift to mature. As a rule of thumb, if your organisation has a relatively warm pool of prospects, you can expect about one in four donors that you cultivate properly to make a significant gift.

That being said, cultivation does need to be taken as a distinct phase before moving into the asking phase – as mentioned previously, many charities stall at this point. Some are guilty of inviting people to wonderful events without sufficient follow-up to the ask. This leaves donors unclear about what is expected of them and gives the impression that the charity has money to burn at prestigious (and costly) gatherings.

In reality, your prospects will have already shown some interest in your organisation either by making a previous gift, perhaps at a lower level, or through a connection with your organisation such as a trustee. You may decide to include others on your lists who have not heard of your organisation. However, your cultivation efforts should initially be focused on the first group who already have some connection with your cause. One senior fundraising practitioner recommends that two distinct groups are invited to different cultivation events, so that you can build on the knowledge of one group and start from the beginning with the others – this way keeps it fresh and some people don't think 'yawn – I've heard this before'!

Many organisations fail to appreciate the value of cultivation activities. Common objections include:

- it takes too long

- we need funding now

- we don't have anyone to help us with cultivation activities

- it is too expensive, and we don't have the budget for events.

These views fail to recognise that cultivation activities help to qualify the value and establish the interest of an individual in your work. Cultivation will enable you to focus on a key group of potential supporters, increasing their understanding and interest in your organisation. This will enhance their confidence in you and stimulate their desire to support you. There is no better shortcut to major gift success.

The most effective cultivation activities involve personal interaction, providing opportunities for feedback and conversation, which allow you to assess the person's reaction or enthusiasm to an idea or proposal. There are other ways to cultivate, as well, which are less personal (and therefore less effective), such as newsletters, the annual report, e-mail updates, occasional letters with information about a project, and research papers from public affairs. *When planning your cultivation activities, it is wise, effective and cuts costs to combine cultivation and stewardship activities.*

Although cultivation needs to be a planned activity, it can also occur unexpectedly. This might be as a result of a favourable news article about your organisation in the local press or through the enthusiasm of a board member or volunteer who inadvertently meets a prospect. Cultivation often involves interacting with the many different facets of your organisation and highlights the need for you to consider the motives of the people who represent you, the consistency of messages across your organisation, how responsive and integrated your communication channels are, and the clarity of your organisational priorities across your many stakeholders.

> 'We've worked hard to get everyone on board with this type of fundraising, all the way to the top of the organisation. A major donor might walk in off the street, so we've had to develop a recognition that we're always on show.'
>
> – Alzheimer's Society

Planning Your Cultivation Programme

A systematic programme is required to monitor and plan prospect cultivation. This is because the process is often long and complex and is divided into multiple steps. You will need to consider:

• Available resources both in terms of staff and budget. (If you are a Model One organisation with limited resources and staff time, you will need to ensure you do not undertake more than you can reasonably manage.)

• How attentive your organisation is generally to its donors and therefore the intensity of cultivation activities required.

• The number of prospects to be tracked. This will help you determine the complexity of the system you may require to manage and track your prospects.

Establishing a System to Monitor Cultivation Activities

Dividing your prospect list into meaningful clusters will help to prioritise and plan cultivation activities. As we identified in Chapter Two, you will have already ranked your prospects according to *capacity* to give and *propensity* to give. Those with the highest personal rating will receive the most personal and intensive cultivation activities.

You need to establish a system to monitor *where each donor is within the cultivation cycle*. This will help you identify the donors that need extensive cultivation and those who are almost ready to make a gift. This can be achieved by creating a simple coding system (such as in Table 4.1) and storing this information on your database, an Excel spreadsheet, or on the donor's individual cultivation plan.

TABLE 4.1 DONOR CULTIVATION STATUS

F	E	D	C	B	A
Time unknown/no reason to give	General cultivation (8–12 months)	Focused cultivation (3–8 months)	Ready to be asked (0–3 months)	Considering a proposal	Gift closed/ Stewardship phase

Most organisations will be able to use their fundraising database to track and manage their major prospects. However, a simple system can also be designed using Excel spreadsheets.

The Lightbox, a gallery and museum in Woking, Surrey, is an innovative community museum that was built following a £7 million capital campaign. Marilyn Scott, who oversaw the project, explains how the museum managed its prospect lists.

> 'We have four lists in Excel where we're managing about 300 contacts. We have an *active list* – which includes those we've asked or are about to ask and people that we've got good contacts with. We review this list at a weekly meeting to decide what the next action is for each prospect. We have a *sleeping list*. On this list, we know they have potential, but we don't yet have a link. We're always asking "Do you know XYZ?", with the aim of eventually finding a link. We have a *donors' list* of those who have actually given, and finally an *unsuccessful list*, where people get moved to if we've received a "no". There is a column which allows us to track what they've been sent.'

The Moves Management® system described in Chapter Two will enable you to track the interaction a prospect has with your organisation, moving each donor to the next activity in a good time frame. Ensuring that each step is systematically recorded in your database is critical to good donor management. The objective of this system is to enable you to call up at any time your best prospects and see where you stand with them.

> 'Prospects are reviewed on a regular basis. Our database is essential. We can pull out a portfolio of prospects or run a report at any time. If you did this without using a database, you'll guarantee that the list won't be complete. A good prospect tracking system in your database is essential.'
>
> – The London School of Economics

The five I's

Gill Jolly from Merlin Fundraising Management Consultants Ltd uses the five I's as a useful process to consider when thinking about cultivating the support of your donors.

- Identify
- Interest
- Invite
- Inform
- Involve.

Researching Your Prospects

Cultivation requires you to appreciate the individual in the round. This includes keeping up-to-date with your prospect's family, business, and personal interests, commitments and circumstances. Dedicating time to research is essential. Research includes desk research, using online and printed publications, but also anecdotal research, by asking others who may know the individual.

Be fully prepared and briefed on the individual before meeting him or her personally or at an event. Have a clear purpose for the meeting based upon your research. If you are holding an event, assign staff or volunteers to each prospect. This may be your only opportunity to find out about the prospect, and it must not be wasted. Staff and volunteers should be asked to note items of interest in the conversation (from links to your cause, to people they know), and this information should be captured soon after the meeting or event and added to the prospect's record. When meeting in a small group or one-to-one, it can be off-putting or distracting to you and the prospect if you are writing notes. As soon as the meeting has finished, quickly write down the key findings and actions.

Be aware that staff and volunteers can sometimes be anxious about meeting people they do not know. Sharing what you know about the individual and establishing a clear remit for a discussion with the prospect will ensure your staff member is confident and clear about what the organisation requires as an outcome from the conversation. After each cultivation activity, you should regroup to establish your next move.

ActionAid supports staff by giving them the following guidelines on talking to people at events (see Figure 4.1).

FIGURE 4.1 BRIEFING NOTES FOR A CULTIVATION EVENT (ACTIONAID)

Key points about ActionAid and Ambassadorship

- AA's aim is to eradicate poverty
- AA is one of the UK's leading overseas development organisations
- We tackle poverty's fundamental causes - not just symptoms, helping bring about sustainable improvements to people's lives
- 30 years of experience working with communities and influencing governments
- Activities in over 40 countries reaching 13 million people
- Long-term and trusting relationships at the grassroots and credibility with decision makers
- We are different to other charities because you will get real feedback from real people
- Country Programmes are mainly run by country nationals
- **New strategy – people 'claiming' their rights. Still *fighting poverty together***
- AA aims to give people the opportunity to identify their own problems and shape their own solutions.
- Mention Internationalisation if apt
- **Ambassadorship gives people the opportunity to be on inside track and gain a deeper understanding of the reality of life in the world's poorest communities** (see pledge card for more details)

Involvement with ActionAid and other charities
- o **How long have you supported AA?**
- o **What initially prompted you to get involved?**
- o Is there any area of our work you are particularly interested in? (Introduce them to anyone who can tell them more about this area)
- o Have you been to any developing countries?
- o Do you support any other charities?
- o What's your favourite charity?
- o What would AA have to do to become your favourite charity?
- o **Do you know about the Ambassador Network? (Introduce to Ambassador Team).**
- o Would you be interested in getting more involved? (careful what you're offering!)
- o **Tell them why you love working at AA**
- o Find out what networks they are hooked into that may be useful to us.

What we want from the evening?

- **As many people as possible to sign up to Ambassadorship on the night**
  - o **Opener - 'So what do you think about the speeches?**
  - o **Have you had a chance to think about Ambassadorship?'**
- **Commitment from donors for some kind of follow-up. This could be:**
  - o **Invite guests in to Hamlyn House to meet Richard Miller, one of the Ambassador team, and opportunity to meet some key staff from overseas**
  - o **More detailed meeting with programme staff**

How do I move on to the next person?
- **Introduce them to someone near by and excuse yourself from the conversation**
- Introduce them to someone who may have similar interests
- **Find a staff member who can tell them about an area of work they are interested in**
- **If it's not clear what they're interested in – ask!**
- **Introduce them to an Ambassador who can say why they are so committed to AA**
- It's perfectly reasonable that the home team (particularly fundraising staff) need to talk to as many people as possible. **You will not offend people by moving on. It's your party and you have to talk to everyone!**

What if people ask why they got invited?
- o We have selected a number of supporters who have given more support than most donors
- o We have invited people who live within easy reach of London (we have actually invited people from across the UK – so check where they come from first!)

- **If you get asked a question you don't know the answer to, try to point them in the direction of someone who can answer their question. Alternatively, say we'll get back to them with an answer and let one of us know.**

Identifying Necessary Support

As we saw in Chapter Two, cultivation activities require *people* and *budgets*. If your organisation is serious about developing a lasting relationship, it must be prepared to invest in cultivation activities by making an appropriate budget available.

Different groups of people can support your cultivation efforts. These include operational staff, chief executives, trustees, volunteers, and donors. By assigning different cultivation activities to people within this network, you will easily be able to develop an annual programme making the best use of available resources.

This might include:

• assigning five major donor prospects to each board member and your chief executive, allowing them to take the lead in cultivating a small group of individuals

• asking a volunteer or trustee to host a cultivation event at his or her home

• using volunteers to share their enthusiasm about a project with a potential prospect at lunch meetings

• organising an annual informational briefing in your office or at one of your projects, inviting key people to share your vision for the future

• involving staff in project or office visits. Inform them that the prospect is visiting, how long this will last, what you would like them to say or not say, and ensure you let them know about any positive result further to the visit.

If you plan to assign volunteers such as board members to cultivate a group of prospects, consider drafting a short list of responsibilities, explaining what is expected when contact is made. It is important to emphasise that the relationship with any prospect must remain with the organisation, and while friendships may develop, they must not be at the expense of the organisation's relationship. Don't be too disappointed if only one or two trustees offer to help; you will have already made a big difference in your ability to cultivate donors.

Developing Cultivation Plans for Your Key Prospects

Once you have identified your key major-donor prospects, you'll need to develop a plan for their cultivation. This may range from making personal contact twice a year to a comprehensive and detailed plan of action, such as in the following cultivation plan from The Woodland Trust. The plan highlights how a programme of activity is developed to draw the prospect closer to the organisation.

The prospect is 'owned' by one individual, who is the lead fundraiser for the contact. This establishes accountability, and this individual is responsible for managing the relationship with the prospect, providing the initiative and strategy. This would normally be a member of the staff, who may utilise other members of staff, board members and/or volunteers to help develop the relationship.

To commemorate the bicentenary of the Battle of Trafalgar, The Woodland Trust, the UK's leading woodland conservation charity, teamed up with the Society for Nautical Research and HMS *Victory* to launch a fundraising and awareness campaign to create commemorative woods and educate people, especially children, about the link between trees, timber and our maritime past. Donors were invited to adopt areas of woodland named after one of the 33 British ships at the Battle. Table 4.2 relates to this campaign and maps the step-by-step cultivation of a particular donor.

TABLE 4.2 MAJOR DONOR CULTIVATION PLAN

Prospect Name	Lead Fundraiser	Date Updated
Mrs Y	Sue	September 2011
Source	Potential Ask	Likely ask date
Business contact	£50K +	Spring 2012
Solicitation Stage		
6		
Natural partners		
Her business connections		
Case for support		
Has been Trafalgar Woods, not sure what next. Ancient trees? Children/young people? Corporate approach to business? Regional project?		
Lead Project/s: Trafalgar Woods until 2012		
WT Staff: Sue, Karl and CEO		

Next few moves		
Action	Deadline date:	By whom:
Met via X at invitation to dinner, which was accepted. It turns out Y is a keen Nelson enthusiast. We already knew she was a keen sailor. Who else do we know involved in sailing?	Jan 2011	Sue.
Sent copy of sailing book	Feb 2011	Sue
Invited to follow-up event: declined	May 2011	Sue
Sent update as part of follow-up. Y made donation of £10k for Trafalgar Woods from her CT (previously unknown to us)	June 2011	Sue
Invited to Wood ceremony. Turned down by letter from PA.	September 2011	Sue
Research CT – size/criteria?	September 2011	Dilys
Research opportunities for support from within company owned by Y and prepare a proposition	October 2011	Jason
Invite/inform about community/schools planting at Trafalgar Woods in November	End of Oct	Sue
Send photo and update report following woods ceremony	Nov/Dec 2011	Sue
Arrange face-to-face meeting (ideally locally) e.g. visit to Chatham Historic Dockyard	Jan/Feb 2012	Sue
Invitation to gun deck dinner on board HMS *Victory*, include personal note from Project Patron	March 2012	Project Patron
Send Y CEO report highlighting key achievements and plans for Trafalgar Woods project	April 2012	CEO
Face-to-face ask as follow-up to the dinner	May 2012	To be decided

All of these 'moves' are based on the prospect's attendance and interest in each step. The plan may change as visits uncover new things about the individual. After attendance at two or three meetings or events, you would have a good idea about how the prospect feels about the campaign and the proper way to solicit him or her. A plan such as this should be developed for your lead prospects.

Regular reporting

When a number of staff or volunteers are assigned to lead on the cultivation of specific prospects, regular reporting and feedback are necessary. This may range from asking staff to provide feedback on approaches made to their top 10 prospects at a team meeting to holding a monthly or quarterly prospect review meeting where the information can be updated, the next moves planned, and any difficulties discussed.

Ways to Cultivate Your Donors

Cultivation is strategic, and therefore it needs to be planned. It includes activities that are aimed at a 'collective' group of donors and which might be mapped out on an annual calendar of events, and 'individual' activities that are tailored to the prospect. In every organisation, there will be methods and opportunities for cultivation – all that may be required is some imagination.

You should start by identifying cultivation opportunities that are accessible and easy to implement within your existing programme of activities. Develop a calendar of activities, ensuring they are well-paced like the ones in Table 4.4.

You should consider:

• *collective* activities that cultivate donors in a group, such as 'information' events

• *individual* activities, usually employing one-to-one opportunities tailored to the individual donor.

Each activity should work to *educate and engage*, increasing the understanding of your work and portraying your organisation as successful, important, and effectively run.

Different donors seek different things from their involvement in your organisation. For some, this may mean placing an emphasis on the results of your organisation in your community. Others may be interested in the financial performance of your organisation or in peer association and high-level networking opportunities. Ultimately you are trying to engender a sense of their ownership of your organisation, which leads to a sense of responsibility for its wellbeing and an obligation to help. Only by meeting and getting to know your donors will you be able to establish their motives and tailor your next moves accordingly. Your programme therefore needs to be flexible and *offer a range of activities to suit different audiences*.

TABLE 4.3 EXAMPLE CALENDAR OF CULTIVATION ACTIVITIES

Activity	Q3 Oct–Dec 2010	Q4 Jan–Mar 2010	Q1 Apr–Jun 2010	Q2 July–Sept 2010	Q3 Oct–Dec 2010	Q4 Jan–Mar 2011	Q1 Apr–Jun 2011
Cultivation events							
Sheffield							
Birmingham							
Bristol							
Barnsley							
London			Bank of England		WSD Artwork	London Eye	
New eye 2 eye regions							
SeeAbility Carol Concert							
Volunteer Leadership events	Bisley (JD)		Bristol (SR)		London (RR)		Other (TBC)
Key Donor Communications							
Personalised Christmas card							
Annual donation anniversary letter							
World Sight Day Communique							
Interim eye 2 eye report							
Annual Review							
SeeAbility's Birthday							
Ambassadors							
Annual Ambassadors lunch			SeeAbility B-Day		WSD		SeeAbility B-Day

Cultivation Techniques

This section includes a range of cultivation techniques with examples from different organisations.

1. Personal meetings

The most effective method of cultivation is face-to-face meetings. This is time-consuming and requires planning and preparation and a commitment from the organisation's leaders, whose attendance will frequently be required at meetings or events. However, when done well, the return on investment typically will be high. Personal visits can take on a variety of forms. It is essential that they are well-planned, that staff and volunteers arrive on time, and that a clear purpose for the meeting has been established. This level of preparation signals to your prospect that the meeting is important to you.

Face-to-face meetings might include:

• a private meeting at the prospect's home, taking advantage of the opportunity to introduce yourself as a new member of staff

• a visit to your organisation or project so that the prospect can see firsthand the work you do and experience the passion of your staff. Consider bringing someone with you who has already made donations and believes in your organisation

• a lunch meeting with an enthusiastic volunteer or board member who gives an update on your programmes.

2. Opportunities for involvement

Cultivation activities that invite involvement shift the relationship with the prospect from a reactive one, where the individual responds to an opportunity for participation or information, to one where the individual is required to take action on behalf of the organisation. This shift encourages the prospect to participate in your cause. Involvement also allows you to encourage questions or objectives that the prospect may raise. For these reasons, a calendar of cultivation activities for individual prospects should include opportunities for involvement.

'We organise reunions for our alumni. There is also a lecture series run by the School – we're fortunate because it is a *candy store* of opportunities with up to three lectures per week. We also arrange lunch with academics.

'We have a high-level campaign committee, who are volunteers. They are a sub-set of the board with a remit to support our appeal. Each of them has made a personal gift. One of them has been host to a party in his home, which gave us an occasion to invite modest donors, or those who had done something for LSE. It gave us a way to elevate people – through the exclusive venue.'

– The London School of Economics

• Ask for their advice about a new or proposed programme or project by sending them a proposal in advance of a meeting.

• Send a questionnaire to ask about their preferences and provide feedback on your organisation (taking care to personalise it so that it doesn't appear to be a 'mass-marketing' technique).

• Ask them to volunteer or join a committee or working group within your organisation to use their specific expertise.

• Invite them to participate in a focus group or join an interview panel for a senior post.

• Write a feature story about the donor for your newsletter or website. This will inspire others and bring your donor closer to your cause.

• Ask them to submit a quote and photo for your annual report or website about their experience with your organisation, their interests, or business background. Send them a copy with a personal note.

• Ask them to lend you something. This might include a painting for an exhibition, or their home or office for an event.

• Invite donors and prospects to speak at your event or conference or to join a panel discussion to share their experience of your organisation or their specialist area.

• Invite them to be a member of your organisation. Joining an organisation helps a donor to recognise that he or she has made a commitment to it.

• Invite them to a presentation or discussion about the future of your organisation.

An increasing number of organisations are finding that donors who campaign give more. Many organisations now use campaigning messages to engage people in the cause. The Friends of the Earth campaign, The Big Ask, invites potential supporters to take action, which helps to strengthen the donors' bond with the organisation.

FIGURE 4.2 'THE BIG ASK' CAMPAIGN BY FRIENDS OF THE EARTH

Case Study: Capability Scotland

Capability Scotland is Scotland's leading disability organisation, providing a range of flexible services to support disabled people of all ages in their everyday lives.

Once a year, Capability Scotland holds a 'Chief Executive's Lunch' for 20 of its top donors and prospects. The lunch is held in a boutique hotel, where the food and wine are donated.

The lunch is a way of the organisation's chief executive saying, 'We've selected you as special friends to talk to about our plans.' It's a working lunch. We'll report on how far we've progressed during the year; for example, this time last year, we said X, whereas now we can report Y. There's an introduction saying why the group has been invited, and it provides a way of making sure that those closest to our organisation feel they have privileged information. It is a way of engaging and involving them in our work.

Everyone is made to feel very special, there is no ask and no pack that people are sent home with.

– Capability Scotland

3. Engage their connections

People tend to be flattered when asked for their advice. You may seek the help of a prospect by asking for his or her expertise, contacts, or influence. A prospect who helps to steer your organisation to a useful contact or a winning grant application is likely to derive personal satisfaction from being a catalyst of success. Keep the individual informed during the process, even if unsuccessful, as the goal is to make this person feel he or she is part of the team.

> 'We're working with a cold prospect who is a technical design expert. We're approaching him and asking him if he'll help us design and build a school. We want this to be the masterpiece – the inclusive design that will then be rolled out across the country. We're asking him to get his friends together and fundraise for it.'
>
> – Scope

• Ask the individual to introduce you to an important contact.

• Ask him or her to review a list of prospects and indicate those they know personally, or invite them to a prospect screening session with other members of your leadership to brainstorm ways of cultivating other prospects. Hold your session at the end of the day, making it informal with wine and snacks.

• Find out if the individual sits on boards of prospective foundations or corporations and can use influence to leverage support for your organisation.

• Ask for the individual's opinions or ideas about what your organisation does.

4. Hold cultivation events

Cultivation events range from large open-house events at your head office to small intimate dinners in special locations. The type of event will depend on its purpose and the prospects you are targeting. If you are seeking to engage a group of prospects who have not yet given to your organisation and have had little involvement, you may need to identify a distinctive venue or special host to attract your audience.

Be clear about the purpose of your event. Is the aim to introduce new people to your work? Do you need to celebrate the success of your organisation, and therefore invite donors to renew their support? Will you ask people to pledge on this night, or follow up with guests afterwards?

It is essential to ensure that your event serves to educate and engage guests in your work so that they will want to invest in your future. Often this involves inviting beneficiaries to talk about their experiences. You must also ensure that there is appropriate follow-up. Without systematic follow-up based on an identified cultivation plan for the individual, events are likely to be ineffective.

Tips for a successful cultivation event:

• Establish a clear purpose for the event.

• Identify a venue that is unusual or inaccessible to the public.

• Keep the event small and exclusive to allow you to talk to each attendee.

• Meticulously plan the details with the donor in mind; consider timing, seating plan, name badges, parking facilities, etc.

• Identify ways of creating a buzz about the event; for example, calling your key prospects before they receive the invitation.

• Assign each guest or table to an appropriate member of staff or volunteer who is briefed on the specific outcome required, e.g. to ascertain information or to ask for a meeting or introduction.

• Invite beneficiaries or develop a strong presentation that brings your work to life.

• After the event, debrief your staff and volunteers to capture relevant information and identify follow-up actions required.

• Undertake swift follow-up with personal phone calls or letters of thanks.

Case Study: Celebrity Pledge Dinner for ActionAid

The dinner we held with a well-known actress was an exclusive dinner with 14 donors. We held it at a private club where this actress is a member. She hosted the dinner and paid for it. It was a pledge dinner, and people were asked to pledge on that night. We made it clear that we were asking for money at the dinner. There were no specific amounts sought. On that night, we generated £80,000 in pledges in total. Some people gave later, and we subsequently received a total of £150,000. The actress sent a handwritten letter to thank people after the event. Staff then followed up and wrote to thank people for their pledges, saying that we looked forward to receiving them by X date. If you're using a high-profile person, you need to ensure that they are very familiar with your work.

Case Study: Introductory Dinner for The Lightbox, a community gallery and museum in Woking, England

We were given the use of a historic house for a dinner for 60 people. We invited a group, taking the lead from the appeals committee, and added names from our own research. At the event, we provided an introduction to the project – it wasn't a hard sell – but explained that we were seeking 'Founder Sponsors' to fund the project at £10,000 each. During the drinks, we made a presentation outlining the benefits of the project and discussed the architecture of the building itself.

A member of the appeals committee was present at each table. Their role was to engage people at the table. We followed up the event with a feedback session to work out who were our key targets. We are now working with the committee members to follow up these individuals with meetings. We go with them to the meeting, as it's better for two people to attend. If you have two people, one can be more silent and observant, while the other can do the talking.

Often we find that we're not in a position to make the ask at the first meeting. This is usually an introductory meeting, which we use to gauge the interest of the prospect. We leave a document which outlines the benefits of being a Founder Sponsor and a range of opportunities ranging from £10,000 to £50,000.

Case Study: Business Breakfasts for the British Heart Foundation

We've hosted two business breakfasts – one by the chair of our appeal, and another by a member of the committee who works for a leading investment bank in the City. The format for these events tends to involve the host's inviting his warm contacts, and one of the professors whose work we're funding is invited to talk about the programme. These have generated good income with an average donation of £1,000.

5. Personal communication

Providing regular and personalised information is another cultivation technique. Review the information to ensure that it is conveying the message that you want to portray and that it demonstrates the impact and results of your work. As with stewardship reports (covered in Chapter Six), information used in cultivation activities should include quantitative data, such as finances raised or expended and leverage achieved, and qualitative data, which bring the work of your organisation to life through personal stories, testimonials, and photos.

Consider the following:

• Developing a personalised e-mail list to keep prospects up-to-date with a bit more information than you find in the regular newsletter.

• Sending a quarterly personalised letter from your chief executive or chairman, which shares important information beyond your regular communications. This might include recent successes or awards, accomplishments of members of your board, and involvement of other major donors.

• Sending greeting cards for Christmas, birthdays, or special occasions, such as family weddings or grandchildren. Ensure that your chief executive adds a personal note.

• Sending personal notes or e-mails or making phone calls about a forthcoming event or activity.

• Calling donors to see how they are. Ask your chief executive, trustees, or volunteers to help by dedicating time to call and update prospects and thank them for their interest and involvement in your work.

• Clipping and sending an article that is of known interest to them.

6. Provide recognition

Recognition serves to reinforce the donors' involvement and commitment to your organisation. Building this sense of kinship is an objective of cultivation techniques. (Recognition is a topic that is addressed fully in Chapter Seven.)

As part of your cultivation activities, you may wish to consider:

• developing a club, recognition society, membership programme or development board to increase opportunities for communication and a sense of belonging to your organisation.

• identifying naming opportunities or other mechanisms for giving visibility to the people who make your work a reality.

• printing a list of supporters to include in your newsletter or annual report. Seeing a name listed creates affiliation to your organisation and serves as an inspiration to others. Be sure to get their permission – when asking, why not use this as an opportunity to cultivate them?

Getting a 'Yes'

The hardest part of cultivation is getting through the door in the first place. How do you maximise the success of achieving a prospective donor's agreement to a meeting or attendance at an event? This can be especially difficult when there is no link or contact with the prospect. See the sample letters later in this chapter for examples of different approaches.

> 'A lot of people aren't that willing to see you. You might need to be creative; for example, we targeted someone at a seminar, because we knew he would be there, so we bought tickets and went along and said "Can we come and see you".'
>
> – Scope

Here are some tips on ways of increasing your chances of getting a 'yes':

● Don't rush in. Be patient, and build up your contact slowly.

● Wait until you have an introductory contact who has a good relationship with your prospect to help you open the door. Depending on how well your contact knows the prospect, he or she might call the prospect and arrange for a personal meeting, write an introductory letter, or send a note accompanying your letter. Follow-up should be made within one week to ten days either by you or your contact.

● Send a letter from you or your chief executive giving an update, expressing thanks for any support received, and asking for a brief meeting. A formal letter is harder to say 'no' to than an unknown voice at the end of a telephone line.

● Use the telephone only if you have recently been in touch with the prospect or if he or she regularly makes a donation to your organisation.

● Make sure you have the prospect's phone number if you are intending to call him or her to follow up a letter. Be prepared with a list of dates and times.

● Ensure that the individual assigned to the prospect is the person making the call or writing the letter. It is more effective in building relationships to provide continuity by assigning a single contact.

● Make friends with the prospects' personal assistants, as they have enormous powers of persuasion.

> 'Whether it's the prospect's personal assistant, partner or someone else that has influence in the prospect's life, treat these gate-keepers with kid gloves and get them 'on side' first. Based on how you interact with them, your efforts to cultivate a new relationship may rise or fall. Too often, a pitch is made to the male in a relationship, when the female partner may in fact be the one who researches your organisation and makes the final decision regarding whether to donate – and how much.'
>
> – The Community Foundation for Ireland

● Stay in touch, even if you initially receive a 'no'.

> 'Don't give up on people. One donor was impossible to get hold of by phone, but we finally got through.'
>
> – Friends of the Earth

When Is the Right Time to 'Ask'?

'We went to see a lady at her house. She had never given significantly, but when we arrived, she immediately reached for her cheque book. I said 'no,' that we didn't want a donation yet. She then came in to meet the project staff and subsequently gave £10,000. It's really important to wait for the right moment.'

– ActionAid

There are no hard-and-fast rules to knowing when the time is right to make the 'ask'. Unlike gifts from trusts or corporations, individuals don't provide us with deadlines. Instead, you should trust your intuition and let this guide you to 'sense' when a person is ready. It is worth mentioning that the prospect will have the expectation of an ask; if they are well-off, they will be aware of why they are being courted.

Clues will include:

- attendance at several events or meetings over a period of time

- increased interest in your organisation or a particular programme

- increased involvement by offering advice or as a volunteer

- interest in the conversations you and others have with the prospect or donor about the vision and plans of your organisation.

The key, though, is not to leave it too long; be clear about what you want from them or they will give significantly to another organisation who they thought had a greater need as they asked them sooner!

Conclusion

Organisations that are serious about building support for the long term place the concept of cultivation at the centre of their entire fundraising programme and not just with the major gift programme.

Cultivation is a programme of personal interaction between your organisation and your prospects, with the purpose of building their interest, understanding, and ultimately investment in your work. Its primary engine is personal visits, as only through one-to-one discussions can you begin to understand and address personal motives.

It is both an art form and a science. It requires a disciplined scientific approach to systematically monitor and track each move, as well as creativity and flair to decipher each next best step.

Above all, cultivation is relationship-building founded on the principles of genuine respect and appreciation for those with an interest in your cause.

Sample Letters

The following sample letters vary in their style and length; you will need to determine what best fits with the style of your organisation. Use your judgement when it comes to the best way of addressing the individual in the salutation. This will often depend on how well the writer knows the individual.

Sample introductory letter requesting a meeting

Dear Prospect,

I am writing to ask for your advice on something related to my role as chairman of an important national project called the SeeAbility *eye 2 eye Campaign*. The campaign is a flagship project for the charity *SeeAbility* (formerly called The Royal School for the Blind) which I also chair, and which is deeply committed to supporting people with sight loss and additional disabilities and allowing them to lead fulfilling lives.

There are almost 100,000 people in England with a learning disability who are looking but not *seeing* because their eye care needs are not being adequately met. The *eye 2 eye Campaign* outlines an ambitious strategy to ensure that these people get regular eye tests and appropriate low vision support, having a profound effect on their quality of life. We aim to do this by funding 10 community officers and a national information and advisory service.

I want to ask if you would grant me and SeeAbility's chief executive, [name], a brief meeting to discuss possible ways of helping us to achieve our goals for the campaign. To that end, [name] or one of the team will get in touch to organise a date. Alternatively, you can reach me by mobile on [number] or contact [name] at SeeAbility on [number] (direct line) or by e-mail at [e-mail address].

I share with you an e-mail from the mother of a disabled child which illustrates why this campaign is so important.

'My son attended his GP for four years with eye infections, always given antibiotic drops, sometimes without even seeing my

---

son. 12 months ago I took him to hospital, the doctor refused to treat him because of his behaviour, on the way out he handed me again antibiotic drops. Yesterday we went to the hospital, this time a different doctor acknowledged his disability, and examined his eyes. He told me my son was totally blind in one eye and had been for about two years, cataracts had formed because of the constant infection and drops. My son was slowly going blind and couldn't tell me. Can you imagine how that feels as a mother? My son is blind because doctors never saw past his disability.'

I have made my own substantial commitment to the *eye 2 eye* Campaign to ensure that the sight of people with disabilities doesn't continue to be neglected. I hope that you will feel able to grant us a brief meeting and I thank you for your consideration of our campaign.

[name]
Chairman

An introductory letter from a trustee (and owner of a famous New York restaurant) to a prospect

Dear Prospect,

As a fellow supporter of *City Harvest*, I share your appreciation for the incredible work they do bringing fresh food to 260,000 New Yorkers a week. The hunger crisis in New York City is real, and I am proud to join you in fighting this important cause.

For this reason, I would like to invite you for lunch at [X Restaurant] with my fellow board member, [name], and Executive Director, [name]. We want you to learn first-hand how your generosity allows *City Harvest* to do their important work, as well as hearing about recent accomplishments and upcoming plans.

Serving on *City Harvest's* Board of Directors for more than two years has given me the opportunity to make a real difference. It's been a privilege to be a part of a food rescue organization that has long connected New York City's food industry with New Yorkers in need.

I do hope you can come and enjoy lunch with [name] and [name]. [Staff name] will be calling to see if we can arrange a mutually convenient date. Once again, thank you for all you have done to make *City Harvest's* work possible.

Warm regards,
[name]
Executive Chef & Owner, [X Restaurant]

An introductory letter from a staff member

Dear Prospect,

I am writing to introduce myself as the new development manager here at the *Alzheimer's Society*, where my role will be to ensure that our most committed supporters are kept informed and up-to-date whilst encouraging other likeminded individuals to support our work.

As you are one of our greatest benefactors, I would welcome the opportunity to meet with you to update you on our current work and discuss what has inspired your generous support. Any help and advice you are able to give will be of great use in helping me gain a greater insight into how best to meet the needs of our donors whilst furthering the work of the *Alzheimer's Society* and hopefully help even more people whose lives have been affected by dementia.

I will contact you shortly to see whether you are available to meet and to arrange a convenient time and date. However, if you would like to speak to me before then, I can be reached on [number] or at [e-mail address].

I very much look forward to meeting you and would like to take this opportunity to thank you for all your support.

[Staff name]
Alzheimer's Society

Invitation letter to a cultivation event

Dear Prospect,

The Ranulph Fiennes Healthy Hearts Appeal – Business Breakfast

I am helping the *British Heart Foundation* with a major fundraising appeal, aimed specifically at research into heart disease in children. As part of this, I am approaching friends and business acquaintances in the City to see if they would be willing to help. I and my fellow Appeal Committee members have a number of ideas for how you and your company could become involved and contribute to the appeal, and we would like to discuss these with you. We would also like to introduce you to the two prominent doctors, Professor [name] and Professor [name], who are leading the research teams, so that you can hear first-hand how the appeal will contribute to this work. To this end, I would like to invite you to a one-hour breakfast meeting to be held at [prominent city bank] office at 8.30 am on Wednesday, 22 June 2005.

In recent years, the British Heart Foundation has identified three main areas of concern in terms of the heart health and well-being of children and young adults.

1. Congenital Heart Disease: the BHF has been at the forefront of many of the new surgical techniques and treatments that are now used when dealing with a child who has a heart defect. Such has been the success in this field that the figures have been reversed – where previously only one in five children born with a heart defect would survive, we are now in a position where only one in five children born with a heart defect will die. However, this in turn means that around 4,000 children each year will need ongoing help to lead normal lives.
2. Inherited Heart Disease: this area is also known as 'sudden death syndrome' – the heart basically stops. It often involves children and young adults who die without warning and without dis-playing any symptoms. Professor [name] has identified several defective genes which predispose an individual to sudden death, but there are more to be identified, and there is much more work to be done to find out how best to treat people who do carry these genes.
3. Acquired Heart Disease: changes in diet, physical exercise, and other environmental factors have led to an explosion in child-hood obesity – we are now seeing 9-year-olds with a level of damage in their arteries that would previously only have been seen in a 40-year-old.

The medical community, with the help of the BHF, has already begun to understand cardiac disease in young people, but considerable work remains to be done, much of it pioneering research. The teams at the Institute of Child Health (ICH) and University College London (UCL), under Professors [name] and [name], are at the forefront of this effort. The specific aim of the appeal is to raise £2 million for two crucial pieces of technology: a magnetic resonance imaging scanner (MRI) and a catheter laboratory. There is much yet to be learned, and this equipment will have a tremendous impact on the work of these leading research teams.

Leading the public element of the appeal is the renowned explorer Sir Ranulph Fiennes, who will be undertaking an ascent of Mount Everest in the next few weeks, despite having suffered a near-fatal heart attack and requiring double-bypass surgery in 2003. As admirers of Ran, we are very pleased he has agreed to be the appeal president and, equally important, to associate his expedition with the appeal.

[staff name] or [staff name], the appeal administrators, will be in touch with you to see whether you are able to attend. One hour of your time could make a great deal of difference to some very sick children.

I hope to see you on 22 June.

Yours sincerely,

[name]
Committee Member

Sample invitation letter to cultivation dinner

Dear Prospect,

DINNER AT MIDDLE TEMPLE

We are delighted to invite you to a very special event on the evening of Tuesday 12 April 2005. We are thrilled to have the opportunity to hold a dinner at the exclusive Middle Temple.

Starting at 7pm with a drinks reception in the historic Queen's Room, where Her Majesty Queen Elizabeth II stays when visiting, we will then dine in the historic Parliament Chamber, where the governing body meet. The night promises to be an enjoyable and most unusual occasion, in sumptuous surroundings that are closed to the general public.

We would be delighted if you would join us on this very special occasion. Please let [staff name] at Richard House know by 18 March if you are able to accept this invitation. [staff name's] direct line is [number].

With best wishes.

Yours sincerely,

[name]   [name]
President, Richard House Society   Member, Richard House Society

References

Grace, K Sprinkel, *Beyond Fundraising, New Strategies for Nonprofit Innovation and Investment.* John Wiley & Sons, 2005.

Dove, K E, Spears, A M and Herbert, T W, *Conducting a Successful Major Gifts & Planned Giving Program.* Jossey Bass, 2003.

Broce, T E, *Fund Raising, The Guide to Raising Money from Private Sources.* University of Oklahoma Press, 1988.

Fredricks, L, *Developing Major Gifts, Turning Small Donors into Big Contributors.* Aspen Publishers Inc., 2001.

Major Donors; Resource Sheet, NCVO

CHAPTER FIVE

Soliciting Major Donor Prospects

You see, I ask everyone for help all the time. I ask, and I ask, and just when they think they've done enough and are fed up with me, I ask for more. I have no shame.

— *Mother Teresa*

What you'll learn in this chapter

- How to prepare to make an 'ask'
- How to get an appointment with a prospect
- How to conduct the solicitation meeting
- What to do when the meeting is over.

Introduction

We suspect this is the section of the book that most people will turn to first for a quick scan. Hey, we know it's not easy asking strangers for money, but we want you to remember that the people you'll be asking are not strangers; indeed, by this point in the process they should be the most carefully researched and prepared people you'll ever meet. You should know a great deal about them now – from their business to their families, to their charitable interests to the linkage with your organisation. You probably know more about them than they know about you. Because of this, you should feel more confident about making the ask.

Another reason for confidence is because, without knowing it, you've been an unpaid fundraiser for all of your life. We bet that you remember the times you practised your fundraising skills when you asked your parents for the newest Elton John album or the bicycle you had to have. You carefully researched your prospects to figure out where and when to make the ask (you thought, if I ask Dad on Saturday just after he's watched his team win the football match, he'll be in a good mood, more likely to hand over the money, or perhaps it was asking Mum when she had a lot of things going on and would be distracted, thereby increasing your chances). Then you knew exactly how much to ask for and you used your most persuasive argument: 'But Mum, all the kids have bikes!' When you got the answer you wanted (and it may have taken two or three tries to get that answer, having learned by trial and error that the best way to regard 'no' was to think it was 'yes' in disguise), you expressed your gratitude in the most convincing way possible – with a big hug and kiss. You are a born fundraiser.

In this chapter, we'll help you put an adult spin on the solicitation process, starting with preparing to meet with your prospect and moving all the way to closing the gift and knowing what you should do once the meeting is over.

Preparation for the Ask

Once you have completed your research on the prospect (see Chapter Three), you will need to prepare for your meeting. You must have a plan for every meeting you have with your major gift prospects, as well as a planned outcome: do you want another meeting or the opportunity to submit a proposal, or will it be the right time to make the ask?

The Healing Foundation has developed an Honorary Fundraisers' Quick Guide which provides a pocket-sized summary of their case for support and tips of solicitation techniques for their trustees and leadership volunteers.

Preparation meetings with prospects generally fall into two categories:

● *The get-to-know-you meeting.* The first time you meet with a prospect is not the time to ask for a big gift. The prospect needs to know you and your organisation before you ask him or her to consider making a large gift. Be prepared to share information in a general way about the project you think might interest the donor, or offer a tour of your facility, or try to get more information about the prospect, such as who helps make these decisions. Is it the individual's spouse, financial advisor, solicitor, or another family member? Whoever it is, you should include this person in your next meeting. Remember, rushing to ask for a gift will guarantee you will either scare the prospect off, get a donation that is too small, or not ever get a gift.

> 'We were introduced to someone through another contact of the charity and we went to meet him. He'd been invited to a few events but had not attended. When we met him, he said he'd like to make a donation of £10,000 to £20,000. We said 'no,' because he had told us how much he wanted to give to development work, and we wanted to ensure that ActionAid received a bigger slice than he was proposing. It was cheeky, but we wanted him to give a considerable donation. We also felt the ask was too early and that we should wait to bring him closer to the cause. He has subsequently committed £250,000.'
>
> – ActionAid

FIGURE 5.1 HONORARY FUNDRAISERS' GUIDE BY THE HEALING FOUNDATION

The Need

- Over 150,000 patients in England undergoing reconstructive plastic surgery each year
- 14,000 people are admitted to hospitals with serious burns – over half are children
- Over 50,000 new cases of skin cancer are diagnosed in the UK each year
- 600–700 babies a year in the UK are born with a cleft lip and / or palate, making it one of the most common birth defects in the country
- At present no national strategy for research in this area exists

Current Research

- Chair of Tissue Regeneration, University of Manchester, September 2005
- Patient Information Project, Picker Institute, Oxford, September 2003 – August 2006
- Psychological Research Project, Centre for Appearance Research, University of the West of England, September 2005 – August 2008

Mission

The Healing Foundation is a national fundraising charity established in 1999 to champion the cause of people living with disfigurement and visible loss of function by funding research into pioneering surgical and psychological healing techniques. Through research we will also raise awareness about the cause and provide information about the sources of support.

Vision

Our vision is a society where physical and emotional scarring is minimised, physical dexterity is maximised and no one is excluded because of their appearance.

The Costs

- The cost of these projects is £22 million but match funding will provide valuable support. We must raise £12 million from voluntary contributions
- The University of Manchester, where the Tissue Regeneration Centre is being established are putting in £6.95 million worth of support over 25 years
- So far we have raised nearly £5 million

ELEVATOR TEST

(when you only have 30 seconds)

National charity – disfigurement research – wound healing – scars – psychological aspects of disfigurement – from cleft lip and palate in babies through burns, major trauma, reconstructive surgery and skin cancers.

In a phrase: research into disfigurement and visible loss of function.

First Priority Projects
to be Funded

- To establish a National Centre of Tissue Regeneration, a major initiative in the rapidly emerging scientific area of regenerative medicine through tissue growth
- To establish a National Centre in Burn Injury Study, the UK's only academic chair in burn injury study which will become a leading national and international authority
- To undertake a Major Psychological Project to identify what factors predict successful psychological adjustment in people with disfigurement and visible loss of function
- To conduct a Patient Information Project to identify the information needs of patients with disfiguring conditions

There is a range of other substantial projects to complement these headline proposals.

You may have several meetings with prospective donors until they are ready to be asked for a large gift. There is no formula that will tell you just when is the perfect time for the ask. The more prospects you cultivate, the more experience you will get in reading the situation and knowing when the time is right.

- *The cultivation meeting.* The purpose of the next meeting with your prospect is to determine the extent of his or her interest in your organisation. This is the time to be sure you have additional people with you – your CEO, a board member, a staff member, or the person who introduced you to the prospect. The objective of this meeting is to *listen*. Ask open-ended questions such as 'Why do you like our education programme?' and keep quiet – this can be the hard part especially if the asker is nervous. Remind people in advance that they are having a two-way conversation. You are looking for clues as to what motivates the prospect and the level of his or her propensity to make a gift. Be sure to write down everything that happens in this meeting – often prospects will find it off-putting if you take notes during your conversation, so immediately after the meeting, take the time to recapture your memories of it.

You may also have several cultivation meetings. The general rule of thumb: the bigger the gift, the higher the number of meetings that will be required. 'One of the surprising aspects about major-donor fundraising is how long it takes,' says Zoe Macalpine of ActionAid. 'We had a donor that started by giving £5,000. This donation increased to £25,000 per year for a South American project. We recently met with the donor and received a £50,000 pledge for four years, doubling their gift. *It's taken eight years to get to this level of commitment.* It's been a period of learning where we've learnt more about what the donor was interested in and could present options that we knew would resonate.'

Finally, you come to the ask meeting. Congratulations! You've cultivated the prospect to the point where it's apparent the time is right to make *'the ask'*. Now you are ready for the next steps in major gift solicitation.

The next step is to decide who will go to the solicitation meeting. Should it be the CEO, a board member, or another major donor who has made a gift at the same level as the gift you'll be asking the donor to make? It depends. If the prospect has been cultivated by any of the individuals mentioned above, be sure they accompany you at the ask meeting. The most successful asks come from the prospect's peers.

In the US Trust study, affluent respondents listed their preferences in who asks them for gifts. The results are shown in Table 5.1.

We suspect there is a similarity in approaches that should be taken with British major-gift prospects. This means that the development officer

TABLE 5.1 THE APPROACH – DONOR PREFERENCES

Method	Preference
Personal approach by a friend	38%
Letter in the mail	29%
Personal approach by the charity's staff member	22%
Personal approach by a business associate	5%
A telephone call	1%
Don't know	5%

should not really be the one to ask for the gift, although sometimes it's unavoidable. Indeed, we find that when a prospect is asked by a person who has made a gift at the same level (a fundraising peer-to-peer ask), the chances of success are very high.

This brings us to the roles of those who attend solicitation meetings. The ideal scenario would be to have the prospect (along with the other decision-makers), the development officer, and a fundraising peer. The role of the fundraising peer is to open the conversation and close the gift. The development officer's role is to support the fundraising peer by talking about the funding project, having all the facts and figures ready should a question be asked, and to be the charity's ambassador. The fundraiser should also be prepared to discuss options for tax-efficient giving with the donor. These roles should be agreed on before getting to the ask meeting. The fundraising peer and the development officer should role-play with another individual who assumes the role of the prospect. Practising who says what and when will be crucial to the success of the ask. Think through how you might respond when the prospect expresses an objection, or what might happen if the donor is not ready to be asked (despite your best efforts), or what to say and who says it when the donor says 'yes.' This preparation is essential to help your fundraising peer feel comfortable with the process, and this in turn will lead to success which will mean that they will be happy to help again.

A final word on going in pairs to make requests for funds: remember, it is easy for a prospect to say 'no' when you are not asking face-to-face; it is more difficult for one to say 'no' when one is sitting face-to-face, but it is the most difficult thing to say 'no' when one is looking at two enthusiastic ambassadors of an organisation. There is success in having two people who are asking, but it can get overwhelming for the prospect to have three or more. Carefully think through who and how many people are necessary to make the ask.

Getting the Appointment

Possibly the biggest hurdle once you've identified your prospect is to get the appointment. This is the point where it is very easy for a prospect to say 'no' and the point where you will know just how interested he or she is in your organisation. There are several routes to take when trying to get an appointment with your major gift prospect:

● *In person*. This is the best way to ask a prospect for a solicitation meeting. Using the principle that it's very difficult to turn down a request in person, you increase your probability of getting a meeting. The best way to get the meeting is to ask the fundraising peer to arrange the meeting in person, as prospects rarely, if ever, turn down a request from a peer.

● *Using the telephone*. The most common method is to ring up your prospect to ask for the meeting. While this technique may be the simplest, it is the one in which many development officers fail. Why? Because talking on the phone is one of the easiest ways to turn you down – the development officer is a disembodied voice. It isn't possible to see the person so you can't read their body language, furthermore, many people screen calls. If you get a voicemail, don't leave more than three messages over a 3 week period. If you must call for an appointment, don't fall into the second trap – offering only one day and time for the meeting. Right away, the prospect can (and usually will) say 'no.' By offering a selection of days and times, for instance, 'Would either Wednesday at 4 pm or Friday at 1:30 pm work for you?' causes the prospect to see if one of those dates is available. It's a normal human reaction, and before you know it, you have an appointment.

● *Writing*. The best way to use a written invitation is to ask the fundraising peer to write a personal note (not typed) on personal stationery requesting the meeting. But sending a letter to your prospect, asking for an appointment, can also be fraught with disappointment. Now, instead of being a disembodied voice on the phone, you are another step removed with a letter that can be disregarded or lost. If you must write, use the letter to follow up your phone call or in-person request for a meeting. This call can be made by either the fundraising peer or the development officer.

We're often asked where is the best place to meet a major gift prospect. The answer is wherever the prospect wants to meet – the aim is for them to feel comfortable and at ease. The individual must feel comfortable in a setting of his or her choosing; after all, the prospect knows why you are there (if you have done your homework and prepared the person). The worst place to meet, in our opinion, is in a public place such as a restaurant or club. The lack of privacy will often stall a conversation about money. The office can also be a challenge, as the prospect can forestall your ask by answering the phone, checking e-mail, or allowing interruptions from staff. Meeting a prospect at his or her home is a clear sign that you're welcome and that he or she will find your proposal has merit. There are other advantages to meeting at the prospect's home, as it gives you a chance of further 'research' by viewing the home environment which can give clues to interests, family circumstances, etc. Wherever you meet, be aware of your surroundings, and be flexible enough to change your presentation, depending upon the circumstances.

Meeting Face-to-Face

It's Friday at 1:30 pm. You and the fundraising peer are at the prospect's office for your solicitation meeting. Where to begin? Think of this meeting as you might a play – there is the opening act, the middle act, and the final act.

Act I

The opening act consists of breaking the ice, exchanging pleasantries, and getting the prospect to talk about himself or herself. Some of the sure-fire ways to open an ask are to:

- *ask for his or her help.* 'We have an interesting challenge ahead of us, and we'd like to ask your advice in helping us to solve it.'

- *entice him or her.* 'We know your daughter has heart disease. We are working on an important breakthrough which could cure sufferers and we'd like to tell you about it.'

- *ask open-ended questions.* 'What do you think of . . .?' 'How do you feel about . . .?'

- *use narrative philanthropy.* The fundraising peer should tell why he or she is personally involved with your organisation by recounting stories about the people who have been helped by your organisation.

- *sell your vision.* Focus on the impact of what a gift will help you achieve rather than a specific sum of money. Wait for the prospect to show interest.

Act II

The second act is presenting your proposal. This is your chance to make a compelling case for your organisation and your need for support. The development officer can begin to fill the prospect in on the project at hand. Be sure to listen carefully to the donor so that you can tailor your presentation to what you're hearing.

> 'The programmes need to be visionary because this is the type of people we are seeking to attract funding from.
>
> 'Our style is about tempting people into our vision by tapping into the things that make them tick – such as 'you can make a name for yourself'. We've moulded the project pitch to their interests and attention areas.'
>
> – Scope

Give the prospect time to ask questions, and be sure you are listening. If the prospect raises an objection, repeat it to make sure you understand what he or she is saying, and if the fundraising peer can answer it, he or she should do so. Deal with each objection as it arises. Realise that objections are a natural part of the process.

Some of the objections you might hear are:

- I can't afford it now.

- Business is bad, or the market is in a slump.

A potential response might be: 'We'd love to talk with you about other options for making your gift. Perhaps we could stagger the gift over a period of time? Or perhaps we should wait until December to come back to talk with you?'

- Don't you get enough money from the government?

- Your organisation is so big, how would my gift make a difference?

Response: 'The individual donor is our lifeblood. Your gift does make a difference and here's how . . .'

- But I already give to . . .

Response: 'That's wonderful. They do important work, but we address different needs in the following way . . .'

- I just bought tickets to your event.

Response: 'Thank you. You'll have seen something about our work at that event; however, special event fundraising has a high cost associated with it, which is why this gift is so important. One hundred percent of your gift will go directly to fund our work.'

• A peer-to-peer point might be: 'If you give to my organisation, I'll give to yours.'

Response: 'I'd be happy to consider a proposal from your organisation, but that's not why we're here today. I want you to give our proposal the same careful consideration I'll give yours.'

• That's too much.

Response: 'We do understand, and believe us, we don't ask for a gift every day like this. Would you consider making the gift over X year/s?'

• What made you think that I have that kind of money?

Response: 'You have shown tremendous commitment to our organisation/work, and because of that we wanted to come to you first.'

• I'll have to get back to you after I speak to X.

Response: 'We would be delighted to meet with your spouse/advisor so that we can provide first-hand information about the gift. Shall we send some additional materials to X? I can then follow up with a phone call.'

Of course, these are not the only objections you might hear, but they should get you thinking of your own list so that you and the fundraising peer can practise your responses. Remember, there is nothing wrong with saying: 'That's a good question. I don't know the answer off-hand. Let me get back to you.'

Alistair Lomax, Chief Executive of UNIAID, UK suggests there are three types of asks:

• Bulls-eye ask – you know they are ready. The groundwork has been laid and the timing is right.

• Presumptive ask – you assume they are interested in one particular programme or activity based upon your assumptions and research.

• Blind ask of three – you don't know much about them, so you present your vision and then give them three choices, each of which has a different price tag which you may choose to reveal only when they ask.

Act III

The third act is the closing of the gift. You should now find yourselves at the point where the ask must be made. This is a time of negotiation. Come to the meeting with a specific ask amount or a gift range in mind. The question should be either: 'Would you consider a gift of £5,000?' or 'Would you consider a gift in the range of £5,000 to £10,000?' Be aware not to ask for too low an amount, as most people will go for their comfort zone every time.

Once the fundraising peer has made the ask, *be silent*. The first person who speaks loses. Resist the urge to embellish the ask, splutter or jump in – hold your nerve and your tongue! You must let the prospect think and react. We've been involved in asks where the prospect took up to a minute to respond – 60 seconds of silence is nerve-wracking. Don't apologise for making the ask – remember, you are asking on behalf of your organisation, not for yourself.

If the prospect offers an amount that is too small, try to prolong the negotiation by asking if you can check with the chairman of your board to see how a smaller gift will affect the funding needed for the programme, offer an extended payment schedule to increase the gift or review tax-efficient giving options that may help the donor. Remember, it is very difficult to get a prospect to increase a gift once the pledge is made.

The objective with the closing is to get something – the gift, or another meeting, or the chance to present a written proposal. Never, ever leave without getting something, even if it is an appointment to call/meet again. Always keep the lines of communication open and agree the next steps.

When the Meeting Is Over: What's Next?

Hooray! Your prospect has now become a major donor. What now? First, be sure to thank the donor before leaving the meeting. Write thank-you letters, the official letters from your charity, along with handwritten notes from you and your fundraising peer. Again, these all need to be done quickly, including confirming what the donor will receive in terms of 'recognition' if this has been discussed as part of the process.

Celebrate! Be sure to let your chief executive, the board, and your fundraising committee know about the successful solicitation. If the donor agrees, list his or her name prominently on your donor recognition list. You might be able to ask your new major-gift donor for the names of other potential donors, or ask him or her to make calls with you. Don't forget to send the six-month progress report on the results of the gift and arrange a meeting to present the report in person. Try to get the major donor involved with your charity, first on a committee, and then explore the potential of their becoming a board member.

Conclusion

The secret ingredients in successful solicitations include thorough preparation for the ask by the solicitation team; listening carefully and remaining flexible enough to read the situation and change gears if necessary; having a fundraising peer with you at the solicitation meeting; using the phrase 'Would you consider . . .' or 'We were hoping you'd consider a gift in the region of . . .'; remaining quiet after the ask to allow the prospect the opportunity to respond; and walking away from each solicitation meeting with something. By following these basic rules, your organisation will be on its way to achieving your major-gift goal each year.

References

Affluent Participation in Charitable Giving, US Trust Company, 2000.

Fredricks, Laura, *The Ask: How to Ask Anyone for Any Amount for Any Purpose*, Jossey-Bass, 2006

The Major Donors Code of Fundraising Practice, Institute of Fundraising, 2006

CHAPTER SIX

Nurturing Your Donors for Long-Term Success

Friendship isn't a big thing – it is a million little things.

— *Author Unknown*

What you'll learn in this chapter

- The importance and value of donor stewardship
- Acknowledgement: the art of saying 'thank you'
- Communications and reporting in the context of stewardship.

Introduction

It worked! You have identified, targeted, and approached your major donor prospect. Staff and volunteers have been involved throughout your organisation; you have taken careful steps to ensure that every communication presents your case with urgency and impact. And it worked. You have successfully secured a major gift, and an individual has made a significant investment in the future of your charity. Now it is up to you to prove to your donor that his or her investment was wise.

Unfortunately, evidence from donors indicates that they are often left disappointed with the experience of giving, as charities sometimes fail to address the intangible psychological rewards that donors may be seeking from their involvement with a cause. It is crucial to recognise that this is a process of giving *and* receiving. Just as important as understanding motivations for giving is to understand and address what a donor seeks to receive from the act of giving. For many donors, this is the knowledge that their giving benefits society as a whole, providing the 'warm-glow effect'. Others may seek tangible rewards, such as seeing their names displayed on a community project. To work effectively, this needs to be a two-way process, with the organisation achieving its goals and the donor feeling they are valued and appreciated. Many major appeals have been successful in raising their capital sum but then have totally neglected the donors, resulting in failed relationships only to have the organisation try to re-kindle them again in x number of years. This 'stop-start' approach is offensive to donors and time-consuming and expensive for charities.

It is understandable, then, that the act of giving can leave a donor wanting, when his or her passion about the case for support is lost in the wake of a humdrum thank-you letter that sometimes arrives several weeks later. Or when a yawning gap of months exists between one communication and the next, or when previously handwritten notes are replaced by a 'Dear Friend' letter accompanying the latest newsletter. Encounters such as these can amount to an entirely different experience for donors to your charity and can leave them feeling at best unfulfilled and at worst cheated.

Establishing a donor stewardship programme will help to ensure that your donors receive the single most important message: their gifts matter. This conveys clearly that their support – big or small, year in and year out – is the key to helping you reach your goals.

This chapter aims to address the key elements of a donor stewardship programme to help your charity become effective in responding to and managing relationships with your donors for the long term.

Donor Stewardship in Context

The concept of stewardship can be traced back to the Middle Ages, when the steward was charged with the responsibility of protecting the estate of the owner. Stewardship is the process whereby your organisation cares for and protects its philanthropic support in a way that responds to the donor's expectations and wishes. Stewardship is commonly used as a term in the US, but many of us in the UK are less familiar with it. However, it is becoming more widely used and understood and we expect this to increase in the coming years.

Peter Brinckerhoff, in his book, *Nonprofit Stewardship*, notes that starting from and operating within a stewardship framework forces us to keep our organisation's mission foremost and to analyse decisions based upon their maximum 'mission investment'.

In practice, a stewardship programme provides the opportunity to:

• provide an appropriate expression of continuing appreciation and recognition for gifts.

• demonstrate your organisation's ability to apply a gift to good effect on behalf of the beneficiary.

• build credibility and trust in your organisation.

• increase the level of interest and involvement of the donor in your cause.

• solicit larger donations in keeping with the donor's interests.

At the heart of stewardship is trust – building trust in the competency of your organisation to manage its resources effectively.

The principles of a stewardship programme, such as those in the 'Donors' Charter' of the Institute of Fundraising, set out the standards a donor can expect from fundraisers and organisations before, during, and after the processing of a gift.

The Donors' Charter

When you consider making a gift to charity, we undertake that:

- All communications surrounding it will be honest, truthful and will comply with the law.

- Your right to privacy will be respected and you will not be subjected to any form of pressure.

- Your gift will be applied to the purpose for which it was originally requested.

- Your gift will be used in a way that preserves the dignity of the beneficiary.

- Your gift will be handled responsibly and to the greatest advantage of the beneficiary.

- Fundraisers and the organisations that they represent will consider how they meet your wishes as a donor and will be transparent in their dealings with you.

- Fundraisers will respect your needs for confidentiality and will comply with the law relating to fundraising and the use of personal data.

- Fundraisers will strive to achieve the highest professional standards at all times.

Any concerns you may have relating to these points will be handled swiftly and effectively by the organisations with which they are raised.

– Institute of Fundraising

Good stewardship is centred on the interests and needs of the donor, rather than the needs of the organisation.

Staff and volunteers of a charitable organisation are accountable to funders; therefore, stewardship is the responsibility of everyone in the organisation. Fundraisers interested in securing major gifts have a special duty to develop and plan stewardship activities, because, as discussed later in this chapter, these form the pathway to increased donor loyalty, commitment and, ultimately, future gifts.

Donor Stewardship in Practice

Donor stewardship is a series of activities, policies, and procedures that serve as a mechanism to build and nurture lasting relationships between your charity and those who support your work financially.

The three key elements of a donor stewardship programme are shown in the diagram below. These are:

• acknowledgement: understanding the art of 'thank you' through acknowledging contributions in a timely, accurate, and appropriate manner.

• sharing the vision: reporting to donors in a consistent and accurate manner on the use and impact of their financial contributions to the work of your charity.

• recognition and respect: recognising donors in meaningful ways, such as with events, annual reports, and updates appropriate to the donor's wishes. This topic is addressed in detail in Chapter Seven.

FIGURE 6.1 THREE COMPONENTS OF A STEWARDSHIP PROGRAMME

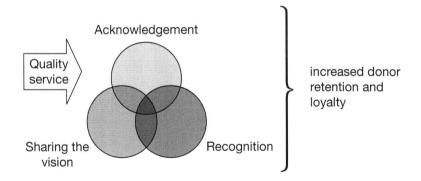

Five Good Reasons to Implement a Stewardship Programme

● Thinking long-term ensures that you are mindful of those donors who may extend their giving through a legacy.

● Building meaningful relationships with your donor will encourage new and larger major gifts.

● Donors who care passionately about your work will share their passion with others.

● It is cost-effective for your organisation, because its outlays to recruit a new donor can be five times greater than costs to secure more funding from an existing supporter.

● When giving is a rewarding experience, it encourages a culture of giving, which benefits not only the organisation but the broader community.

Acknowledging Contributions in a Timely, Accurate, and Appropriate Manner

A good donor stewardship programme will ensure that proper procedures and systems are in place to acknowledge the support of major gifts. An even better programme will use the acknowledgement process creatively as an opportunity to engage the donor in a meaningful way to ensure that donor cultivation is built into each acknowledgement.

Policy and Framework

It is important to establish how gifts will be acknowledged and recognised by your organisation. A policy will ensure that consistency is applied in acknowledging donations now and in the future. You should establish in detail how a gift is recorded, processed, acknowledged, and recognised in your organisation.

A policy for acceptance and acknowledgement of gifts might include:

● how gifts are acknowledged, by whom, and in what time frame.

● the type of gifts your organisation is willing to accept; for example, cash, gifts of shares, property, or valuable items.

● methods of recognition for gift levels and types.

The following policy for the Flagstaff Medical Centre in Arizona is an example of a gift recognition policy. You may also wish to include details about the types of gifts your organisation is willing to accept.

FIGURE 6.2 SAMPLE DONOR RECOGNITION POLICY FROM FLAGSTAFF MEDICAL CENTER

**Flagstaff Medical Center** *Member of Northern Arizona Healthcare*	**FOUNDATION** **Operational Policies & Procedures**	Author: MC/AF
		Effective Date: 9/13/02

Subject: DONOR RECOGNITION POLICY

POLICY: Realizing that the donor, whether individual or corporate, is the crucial element in any giving program, The Foundation for Flagstaff Medical Center acknowledges that importance through the following Donor Recognition Policy:

PROCEDURE

I.   For every gift, regardless of size, a written thank you, hand signed will be sent within three business days after receipt.

o   For gifts of over $1,000, there will be a second letter within one month from the President/COO.

o   For memorials or tributes, a signed card will be sent to whomever the donor requests within three business days after receipt. The Donor will be notified that the memorial or tribute has been received and that the honoree has been notified of same (no amount on honoree=s note).

II   Permanent, public recognition for every donor with cumulative gifts of $10,000, and give permission for the public recognition.

1.   There will be a permanent Donor list in the lobby of Flagstaff Medical Center. Names will appear only with the permission of the donor.

2.   If an individual wishes to open a named philanthropic fund with the Foundation, an initial investment of $100,000 is required. The named fund will be recognized on the engraved Donor list.

3.   All donors who contribute $1,000 or more will receive a phone call immediately to let the donor know the gift has arrived.

4.   There may be an annual reception to recognize all donors who have given at least $1,000 that fiscal year.

5.   There will be an engraved list of those who have signed a letter of intent to remember Flagstaff Medical Center in their estate planning.

6.   Recognition of contributions to specific campaigns will be determined in the campaign plan. In general, permanent recognition will be placed at the site of any new construction or capital project.

7.   Design of any public recognition should be reviewed and approved by the Interior Design Committee. The Board of Directors has final approval of any significant public recognition.

DURATION: This policy will be re-evaluated by the Philanthropic Development Committee every three years beginning in 2005.

The Art of 'Thank You'

Expressing thanks in a thoughtful, respectful, and distinctive way is marketing at its best. The result is a win-win situation in which your donors feel valued and appreciated for their contributions. Such expressions not only show your organisation's gratitude and good manners, but provide you with opportunities to inform donors further about your work and to show them that you care, and to strengthen a relationship. In addition, because donors generally have no contact with the beneficiary, they often judge how effective an organisation is in delivering its services by how well they are treated. Spending time crafting the right follow-up to a donation is a smart investment for the future.

Here are some key considerations.

Be Prompt

Include in your policy an appropriate response time for acknowledgements. Many organisations will place a phone call or send an e-mail to say thank you as soon as a donation has arrived and then follow up with a more formal letter or note. Others will ensure that a thank-you letter is sent the same day.

'We make sure our donors are cared for. As soon as we receive a donation, we write to them immediately, or thank them by phone.'
– British Heart Foundation

Be Personal

Consider how you can make your thank-you warm and personal.

• *Personalise your letter:* add a postscript or personal handwritten comment at the bottom of your letter.

• *Handwrite the envelope:* a handwritten envelope has a more personal feel.

• *Make a phone call:* use the phone for an unexpected, spontaneous thank you. Responding immediately to a gift is less scripted, and your donor is likely to be more surprised by your thoughtfulness.

Methodist Homes for the Aged, a national charity in the UK providing residential care, community schemes, and sheltered housing for the elderly, phones every donor on immediate receipt of a gift of £250 or more.

• *Write in the 'voice' of the author:* consider how you can bring your personality or the personality of the signatory to life through words.

'We pride ourselves on being able to write in various voices – we send a thank you letter from the person. If they say, "we love having your support", that's how we write it. If they are more formal we use that style.'

– Asia Society, New York

• *Consider sending a handwritten note instead of a formal letter:* a handwritten note communicates to donors that they are special and that they are the only ones you are thinking of when you're writing it. It is personal and spontaneous, because you are writing as you think. Consider having a note card designed for your charity that reinforces the work you do.

> A hospice based in Iowa found that handwritten thank-you notes made a significant impact on future gifts. When donors who made a donation of $500 or more received a handwritten thank-you note from the fundraising director, the number of gifts increased to 124 from 103 over a one-year period.

Scope, a UK charity that supports disabled people, has a series of note cards, each one carrying a drawing by a child they support. Key supporters are thanked within 24 hours with a personal handwritten note from the appropriate person.

FIGURE 6.3 HAND-DRAWN CHRISTMAS CARD FROM SCOPE

Be Specific

Illustrate how a donor's gift will make a difference. Consider how you can use both quantitative and qualitative material; for example, a quote from a beneficiary or a specific example of how the funds will be used to achieve change. Be careful here that you don't inadvertently earmark an unrestricted donation.

Be Responsible

The donation must be used for the purpose for which it was given (if this has been specified), and any specific obligations or promises made to the donor must be fulfilled. Respect your donors' wishes for anonymity or acknowledgement.

Be Appropriate

Ensuring that your response to a gift is appropriate is also about knowing your audience. How can you use what you've learnt about your donor to have the greatest impact? Tailor your acknowledgment to capitalise on what is important to your donor. Consider the following.

- *Who is the most appropriate person to thank the donor?* Is this you or the volunteer who helped introduce the donor? Consider who knows the donor best. If you are thanking a donor who enjoys recognition, consider having several people in your organisation respond, including your senior leadership. Thank-you letters ideally should come from more than one person. When you post them, ensure that the letter from your chief executive or chairman arrives first. Asking board members to make thank-you phone calls has the added benefit of engaging them in the major-donor fundraising process, introducing them to donors and gently easing them into asking for a gift.

Donations of more than £10,000 to the British Heart Foundation receive a thank-you letter from the Director General. Donations between £5,000 and £10,000 are thanked by the director of fundraising, and those of less than £5,000 by the major-donor fundraiser.

City Harvest, a group in New York City that provides food to New York City's hungry men, women and children, organises a 'thank-a-thon' each year for their major donors. Board members are assigned a list of donors to call and thank using the following script.

Sample brief for board member thank you calls at City Harvest

For initial comment or voicemail message. Please feel free to adapt this to your own personal style.

Hello, my name is _____ and I am calling as a (volunteer/Board Member) of City Harvest. You have been a donor to City Harvest for some time and we just wanted to call and thank you for your recent gift of $_____, which has allowed us to bring food to so many hungry New Yorkers.

Once again, thank you so much for your generosity.

Should the recipient be receptive to further conversation, you could comment/ask as follow-up:

● Have you heard about some of our new programs? *(fill in with one or more from the list below)*

● Like you, I'm a strong supporter, and I am always interested to hear what people like most about City Harvest . . .

For additional information:

How much food does City Harvest rescue?

● This year City Harvest will rescue almost 20 million pounds of nutritious food – half of it fresh produce. Our fleet of 15 trucks delivers food to nearly 800 partner agencies and programs throughout the five boroughs that help feed 260,000 people each week.

Who is hungry in New York City?

● One in five New Yorkers needed emergency food this year (of whom 30% are children). Programs continue to report more people, especially children and senior citizens coming to them for food.

What are some of your programs?

● Mobile Market – In partnership with the New York City Housing Authority, City Harvest provides residents of the Melrose Houses in the Bronx and the Stapleton Houses on Staten Island with much-needed fresh produce and nutrition information in order to help them lead healthy, productive lives.

> • Harvest Works – Connects New York State farmers who have
> unharvested crops with hungry people in NYC who need fresh
> produce. This new initiative increases access to fresh produce in
> a number of low-income neighborhoods in NYC, while benefiting
> New York State farmers through increased income and access to
> new markets.
>
> • Kosher Initiative – works in much the same way as the rest of
> City Harvest's food rescue operations, only with a focus on meeting
> the needs of clients at our kosher agencies. We work with the Met
> Council, the Orthodox Union and the UJA Federation to actively
> solicit restaurants, food manufacturers, wholesalers and distributors,
> and synagogues to help identify sources of excess kosher food. Last
> year, we distributed 1.5 million pounds of kosher food to help feed
> more than 44,000 people every month.

• *Is it appropriate to send a small gift to donors?* Such tokens can be
powerful reminders and help connect your donors to your work, especially
when these reinforce the involvement of the donor in your charity or when
they are directly linked to your cause. For example, these could range from
a framed photo of the donor's visit to your project or event, or a laminated
bookmark of posters drawn by schoolchildren benefiting from your
community project. As a rule of thumb, a gift should not cost more than
2–5% of the value of the donation. (See page 124 for a full breakdown).

Be Accurate

Misspelling your donor's name or allowing typographical errors can kill the
good intentions of a thank-you letter. Take the time to proofread your
communications thoroughly. Look at every letter to make sure that it is
correctly formatted and attractive. Detail is important. Do note how they
like to be addressed and ensure you give proper regard to titles and
honours.

Four powerful examples of thanks

• *Illustrating the results of a gift.* Staff at The Woodland Trust, a charity
in the UK dedicated to preserving threatened areas of woodland, collect
pictures and stories to build a scrapbook about the woodland that has
been preserved as a result of the support of a major donor. This makes
for a unique and tangible acknowledgement of gratitude.

FIGURE 6.4 LETTER AND THANK-YOU GIFT FROM THE ACTOR'S FUND

For All
Entertainment
Professionals
The **Actors' Fund**
O F   A M E R I C A

December 13, 2005

Dear Mr. ,

I am thrilled to send you this special token of our appreciation for becoming a
member of the Edwin Forrest Society.

Designed exclusively for members of the Edwin Forrest Society by the renowned
Coty Award- and Tony Award-winning designer Donald Brooks, this beautiful
paperweight has been inscribed with your name. All of us at The Actors' Fund are
very pleased with the results of Donald's exquisite design and we hope you will
display it proudly in your home or office. If your paperweight is ever damaged or
misplaced, we will be happy to replace it upon request.

Thank you again for your support of The Actors' Fund and all those that we help each
year. I am,

Sincerely,

Wallace Munro
Director of Major & Planned Gifts

Enc.:

National Headquarters: 729 Seventh Avenue, 10th Floor New York, NY 10019
(212) 221-7300   Fax: (212) 764-0238   www.actorsfund.org

103

- *An inexpensive gift.* Major donors to SeeAbility, a charity in the UK that supports people with multiple disabilities, receive a copy of the organisation's celebrity cookbook. Each page tells the story of someone who has benefited from the charity's work.

- *Tailor-made thanks.* Sometimes 'thanks' is bespoke. A donor at ActionAid, the international aid charity, wanted a plaque displayed at a project in Brazil. ActionAid arranged for the plaque to be placed at the project, photographed this, and sent the photo in a frame to the donor.

- *Imaginative thanks.* A horticulture charity recently thanked a major donor by framing the words 'Thank You' spelled out in a collage of dried flowers and foliage from the project.

FIGURE 6.5 SAMPLE THANK-YOU LETTER FROM CancerBACKUP (now merged with Macmillan).

04 November 2010

Dear ▨▨ ▨▨▨▨▨

We were delighted to receive your recent donation of £300. You have been supporting CancerBACUP for several years now and I would like to take this opportunity to say a sincere thank you for your continued interest in our work. It is the support of individuals, such as yourself, that allows us to continue offering our services free of charge to anyone affected by cancer.

Our cancer information nurses are currently responding to over 4,000 calls to our helpline every month, while our Local Centre nurses respond to over 1,000 enquiries every month from individuals affected by cancer. Since the beginning of the year, we have opened two new Local Centres, one in Torquay and one in Ipswich. In May we launched a second website (http://www.click4tic.org.uk), specifically designed for teenagers affected by cancer, their friends and family. Last year, we extended the freephone helpline by an extra hour, now open from 9am to 8pm Monday to Friday and our groundbreaking *Cancer In Your Language* service, a freephone helpline which allows callers to receive information and advice in over 100 languages via interpreters, is continuing to grow.

We are constantly endeavouring to reach more people and, as the UK's leading provider of cancer information and support, it is our intention to grow our services to meet the increasing demand for accurate, easy to understand information and emotional support. Your generosity will help us to achieve this.

Once again, thank you for all your support.

Yours sincerely

▨▨▨ ▨▨▨▨▨
Head of Fundraising

Sharing the Vision

Reporting to donors consistently and accurately

A wide body of research indicates that one of the main reasons that people give money is to improve the lives of others and to make a real difference. Most people do not give to 'charity': they give to a cause. Charities need to provide tangible evidence that a gift is effecting change, and that the change is contributing to the betterment of lives.

Communicating how a gift has benefited the people you support, your project, or your community and acknowledging the role of the donor in achieving this are central to good stewardship. Effective approaches include special events, donor or project reports, personal visits, impromptu phone calls, and newsletter articles describing what the collective donations have achieved. These provide valuable opportunities for fostering a stronger relationship with your donor and demonstrate accountability.

Maintaining a relationship is also about keeping in touch. Donors will know they are important to you when you keep them informed, especially in communications that are not expected and in which you are not asking for financial support. Therefore, it is important to have a mix of communications with your donors.

An essential component of good stewardship is connecting your donors to the beneficiaries of their gifts and demonstrating accountability through effective and regular communications. This can be done by creating an annual communications plan that includes both informal and formal reporting to deliver year-round communications to your major donors and prospects.

Formal reporting

Organised periodic reporting, which demonstrates responsibility, accountability, and the value created by a donor's investment, is an important activity in donor stewardship. It helps to reinforce that the investment decision by your donor has been wise.

Formal reporting can take the format of a glossy printed report, a simple typed document, or an article in your newsletter or on your website. This type of reporting is a subtle mechanism for setting the scene for future gifts.

Examples of formal reporting include:

- annual general meeting
- newsletter article
- annual report
- donor stewardship reports
- personal visits
- website story
- e-mail.

Informal reporting

Unexpected communications, such as a surprise telephone call, a hand-written note, or a newspaper clipping about an area that relates to your work or the donor's interests, provide opportunities to communicate with your donor and build relationships.

Examples of informal reporting include:

• A phone call from you or a member of your board updating the donor on your work: 'Terrence Higgins Trust makes time to phone their major donors after Christmas for a friendly catch-up conversation.'

• A handwritten note with a newspaper clipping.

• A copy of a letter you received from a beneficiary.

• An e-mail that includes a recent press release or news clipping or informing your donor about a specific radio/TV programme which features your charity/has relevant info. (This is also appropriate in the cultivation process. One fundraiser we know was trying to set up a meeting with a key person and struggling. Then they asked the donor to listen to some programming about the charity on Radio 4. Following the show, the donor rang the fundraiser to arrange a meeting!)

• A photograph with a short cover note. A conservation project sent a picture of the first bee orchid to people involved with the project two years later to show that the site had naturalised and that key species were starting to flourish.

The telephone can be a highly effective tool to engage with your donors informally. It can also serve as a research tool providing an opportunity to gather information about your donors.

A Major-Donor Fundraiser's Perspective

'I find I'll do anything rather than sit and write a letter. I feel passionate and believe in what we're doing, and I want to tell people and share that passion. If you receive a letter, you read it and put it down. But a phone call is a two-way conversation. When you make a phone call, you can ask a question and get an answer immediately. I believe that if you want to know something, you need to ask! And the element of surprise in receiving a phone call works in your favour.'

– Allison Turner, Methodist Homes for the Aged

Key elements of Providing Appropriate Donor Feedback

Depending on whether you are reporting back informally or formally to donors about their investments in your cause, you should consider addressing the following in your donor communications.

- *Donor context:* what is happening close to the donor's home? How will you address the specific interests of your donor?

- *Impact and Outcomes*

New Philanthropy Capital found that less than half (41%) of charities clearly communicated what change they had achieved in people's lives – outcomes. Donors consistently report that the two most important factors in trusting a charity are how the money is spent and what it achieves. Charities need to be able to answer this by communicating impact and outcomes in their communications.

- *Quantitative data* that provide financial accountability and demonstrate impact.
    - Funds credited and expended for the project or area of work
    - Statistics illustrating:
        - achievement of key performance indicators and successes
        - leverage achieved; for example, number of woodlands saved, percentage of referrals helped, annual increases in numbers of visitors, or numbers of signatures received
        - efficiency of project.
- *Qualitative data* that illustrate the gift at work.
    - Quotes, personal anecdotes, and testimonials
    - Case studies, stories of those helped
    - Photos of the project or people helped.
- *Plus points* that give your organisation credibility.
    - Awards or recognition credited to your organisation's work
    - Association with high-profile or well respected individuals or professional bodies.

'I make it my job to visit projects so I can always pull out a story that matches their interests. This is vital. As a major donor fundraiser, you need to immerse yourself in the charity, you have to be up-to-date and be able to quote information and stories. Our job is about keeping the mundane exciting.'

– Major donor fundraiser

FIGURE 6.6 SAMPLE STEWARDSHIP REPORT FROM CancerBACKUP

10 March 2005

Dear ▓ ▓

I am delighted to acknowledge receipt of your donation of £10,000.

Once again CancerBACUP are very appreciative of your generous support of our Benefactor's Scheme. It has been a busy and rewarding year for CancerBACUP, and I would like to take this opportunity to update you on our recent activities and achievements:

- In August 2004, we extended the freephone helpline by an extra hour, now open from 9am to 8pm Monday to Friday. Our telephone systems indicated that substantial numbers of callers were trying to get through after the previous closing time of 7pm. Every year, the helpline responds to almost 50,000 calls.

  [...]

- We are about to embark on a 3-year project to transfer many of our most frequently requested information booklets and factsheets onto audiotape for the benefit of the estimated 10,000 people living with cancer who are blind or partially sighted.

I am conscious that you have not yet had the opportunity to come in and meet some of the nurses involved in delivering our important services. I shall speak to Isaac and hopefully when you are next in the country he will bring you over.

Once again thank you for your generous donation. All of the above cannot be achieved without the generous support from people such as yourself.

Kind regards

Major Gift Development Manager

TABLE 6.1 TEMPLATE TO PLAN ACKNOWLEDGEMENT, RECOGNITION AND STEWARDSHIP ACTIVITIES AT DIFFERENT GIFT LEVELS

Gift Level 1 £ _____ to £_____	Gift Level 2 £_____ to £_____	Gift Level 3 £_____ to £_____
Acknowledgement		
1. Letter from major donor fundraiser	1. Telephone call and letter from Director of Fundraising	1. Telephone call and letter from CEO and chairman
Recognition		
1. List on website	1. List on website	
	2. List in annual report	
Sharing the Vision		
1. Send annual tailored impact report	1. Send annual tailored impact report	
	2. Invite to CEO lunch.	

Considerations

- Give yourself time to gather the appropriate data from your development or operational teams. You may also need extra sign-off time if other departments are involved.

- Consider an appropriate time to send specific reports: anniversary of the first gift, the founding date of your organisation, an awareness-raising day (e.g. 'Make a Difference Day'), or timing in line with your organisation's fiscal calendar.

- Ensure that the details are 100% accurate. A mistake could cast an unfavourable light on your organisation's effectiveness.

- Be prepared to answer questions from donors.

- Consider how you might deliver the information. Could this be done in person or by hand? Might you send it by courier to give an indication of its importance?

- Manage expectations, especially when reporting on aspects that may not have gone according to plan.

Planning Your Stewardship Activities

Consider how you can segment your donors into categories: those who receive monthly communications, who receive information quarterly, and who hear from you once a year.

Consider developing an annual plan using the template below. Don't forget to combine cultivation and stewardship activities where it is prudent to do so.

Conclusion

A major gift should be seen as the starting point and not the end point of a relationship that needs to be developed and nurtured over time, as donors seek affirmation that their gifts have been wisely invested.

We have a duty as fundraisers to ensure that giving is a deeply appreciated contribution to society and that the experience for donors is rewarding and engaging.

Take care to recognise the donor's requirement (or lack of it) for recognition and balance the costs – some people are put off if they think you are spending too much money on thanking/involving them – there is a fine balance at times.

Ensuring that emphasis is placed on the stewardship of donors is an essential step in this process. It will help to distinguish your organisation from one that qualifies for major gifts to one that has winning factors such as inspiring leadership, the ability to allow donors to experience the impact of their giving, and making people feel great about what they've helped you to do.

References

Walker, C and Pharoah, C (eds) *A Lot of Give – Trends in Charitable Giving for the 21st Century*. Charities Aid Foundation and the National Council for Voluntary Organisations, 2002.

Gilchrist, K, *Looking after your Donors*. Directory of Social Change, 2000.

Brinckerhoff, P, *Nonprofit Stewardship: A Better Way to Lead Your Mission-Based Organization*. Wilder Publishing Center, 2004.

Edwards, L, *A Bit Rich? What the Wealthy Think about Giving*. IPPR, 2002.

CHAPTER SEVEN

Major Donor Recognition

Appreciation is a wonderful thing:
It makes what is excellent in others belong to us as well.

— Voltaire, 1694–1778

What you'll learn in this chapter

- Understanding the value of a recognition programme
- Establishing a donor recognition programme for your organisation
- Designing recognition societies or major donor giving clubs.

Introduction

It's the moment we all dread. You answer the phone to hear an irate donor who has just received a copy of your annual report only to find his name is missing. He expresses his disappointment about the missing acknowledgement, and you must carefully explain that his gift this year was just short of the giving level you set for including names in the publication. It's an embarrassing moment, despite your legitimate reasons for this exclusion.

This circumstance could easily have been avoided by publicising how your organisation recognises donors for different sized gifts. Instead, this donor might have made a marginal increase to his donation, and then seen his name listed, correctly spelled and with his permission. Had this been a positive experience, acting as a stewardship activity, it could have been an important step towards cultivating a subsequent gift. It might have encouraged the donor to be a volunteer or an ambassador for your organisation within the community. But in a case such as this, research tells us that dissatisfied customers are likely to tell as many as seven people about their experience.

This anecdote highlights the interdependence of cultivation, recognition, and stewardship activities, illustrating how they need to work in synergy to deepen commitment from your donors to your organisation.

Giving recognition and respect by recognising donors in meaningful ways, such as events, annual reports, small gifts, and updates appropriate to the donor's wishes, is an essential building block to an effective stewardship programme which we discussed in Chapter Six.

The following chart from the National Arts Centre in Canada illustrates how donors are rewarded and recognised at different levels of giving.

FIGURE 7.1 DONORS' CIRCLE PRIVILEGES CHART FROM THE NATIONAL ARTS CENTRE

Donors' Circle Privileges Chart

Donors' Circle Privileges: 2005-2006	$5,000+ Producer's Circle	$2,500+ Director's Circle	$1,500+ Maestro's Circle	$1,000+ Playwright's Circle	$500+ Benefactor	$250+ Sustainer	$100+ Associate	$10+ Friend
Access to Donors' Circle Phone Line (x315)	o	o	o	o	o	o	o	o
Tax receipt for the full amount of your gift	o	o	o	o	o	o	o	o
Personalized Donors' Circle Card	o	o	o	o	o	o	o	
The Donors' Circular newsletter	o	o	o	o	o	o	o	
Donors' Circle calendar of events	o	o	o	o	o	o	o	
Invitation to Donor Receptions	o	o	o	o	o	o	o	
Invitations to select Open Rehearsals and Previews (listed in donor calendar)	o	o	o	o	5	3	1	
Recognition in Prélude, the NAC's House Program	o	o	o	o	once	once	once	
Complimentary tea/coffee coupons at NAC performance intermission bars	7	7	7	5	5	3		
Advance purchase ticket notice (Fall Gala; G.G. Performing Arts Awards; B&W Soirée; Canada Day party)	o	o	o	o	o	o		
Parking Vouchers ($10 value each)	3	3	3	2	1			
Invitation to the G.G. Performing Arts Awards T.V. Dress Rehearsal	o	o	o	o	o			
Access to Circles Express Phone Line (x355 - same day return service)	o	o	o	o				
Le Café reservation service (booked through Circles Express line)	o	o	o	o				
Reserved VIP parking (booked through Circles Express line)	o	o	o	o				
No fee ticket request/exchange service with access to best seats in the house (booked through Circles Express line)	o	o	o	o				
Priority purchase ticket notice (Fall Gala; G.G. Performing Arts Awards; B&W Soirée; Canada Day party)	o	o	o	o				
Access to parking magnetic swipe card (easy in & out privileges)	o	o	o	o				
Access for you and a guest into our Donor Lounge (preshow & intermission)	o	o	o					
Invitations to the "Meet the Artist" Receptions	o	o	o					
Invitations to Artistic Season Launches	o	o						
Host additional guests in the Donor Lounge for pre-performance cocktails	up to 4							
Reserve a premium Box in Southam Hall, subject to availability	o							
Book the NAC's private Theatre Lounge on any performance night for your personal or business functions, coordination assistance provided upon request	o							

NATIONAL ARTS CENTRE
CENTRE NATIONAL DES ARTS

Many charities spend too little time considering how their donors will be recognised for their generosity. Concerns about not having the resources or the funds to lavish expensive gifts or benefits on major donors in exchange for their donations prevent many smaller organisations from addressing the issue. Other groups are convinced that their donors don't want anything in return. This fails to recognise the strategic value of donor recognition, which is part of a long-term strategy to deepen the relationship and involvement of your donors in your work. Recognition is more than a lapel badge or a framed certificate. It is a series of activities that serve to validate the motives of your donors. How you recognise your donors underpins your relationship with them and therefore their potential to make future gifts.

A recognition programme will:

• act as a cultivation activity, providing an opportunity for you to get to know your donor better.

• establish transparency and organise both internally and externally how gifts are acknowledged and recognised, avoiding year-on-year variances, inconsistencies, and last-minute decisions.

• help to inspire others to give, especially when recognition is given within a peer group.

• enable you to maximise the benefits of your recognition programme in advance and therefore optimise its potential.

• avoid common pitfalls by ensuring that you have permission from your donors and know how to spell and list their names correctly.

• work to distinguish your organisation from others.

This chapter aims to address the key elements of donor recognition and how you can use it effectively as a tool to build relationships and engage your donors in the work of your organisation.

Do Donors Want Recognition?

First and foremost, recognition begins with understanding and respecting the wishes of the individual donor. Each individual is different and will have different expectations and needs. For many donors, recognition simply equals a feeling of being appreciated and a small token can go a long way in thanking and building long-term commitment.

The influential work by Prince and File, *The Seven Faces of Philanthropy*, highlights that different donors are motivated by different things. While some donors may desire a press conference to announce their gift, others are serious when they tell you it must remain anonymous. It's therefore essential to know the donors you're working with and to understand their preferences.

This reflects the work by Theresa Lloyd in *Why Rich People Give*, a study of 76 major donors in the UK. Lloyd found that most people did want some form of recognition, but that the spectrum ranged from those who wanted a private expression of appreciation to those who wanted public acknowledgement. Her work found that many donors considered recognition to be a bonus 'rather like a courtesy present wrapping service for an expensive gift', and that it was the recognition of having made a difference rather than the recognition for just giving that was critical.

Lloyd also found that people wanted to be included in lists of donors, and that this was linked to a desire to be recognised by their peers as a contributor to organisations or to encourage pride in their children. She concludes that donors do want to be appreciated and acknowledged, and that if charities offer a mechanism for recognition, then most major donors do not wish to be left out. Lloyd's findings and a number of other research studies challenge the generalisation that the British demonstrate reticence when it comes to public acknowledgement.

Donors will be more likely to value and appreciate recognition if they are encouraged to see it as a way of inspiring others to give. Lord David Sainsbury, a leading British philanthropist, in an interview for Allivida, an international development organisation, stated: 'I think it's good for the field of philanthropy that there is recognition, as in any other field, when things have been done which have been effective and worked well.' In comparison to America, he said, philanthropy in the UK tends to have a low profile. 'In America, people will automatically think that if they have made a lot of money, a proportion of this should go to charity. We're beginning to move towards that in the UK, but there's still a long way to go. And anything that encourages people is a good thing.'

The key is to remember why recognition is valuable – to retain the donor. This requires planning to establish mechanisms and a careful balance of activities but also flexibility to enable you to tailor activities to your donor's preferences.

Design Considerations for Your Recognition Programme

Establishing a framework and policy for your recognition activities in advance can save time and money and allow you to support your major donor programme more effectively. Here are the key steps to consider:

• Establish measurable objectives for your programme; for example, the number of donors you wish to generate at each level, and whether you aim to secure an increased number of gifts above a specific level or to retain donors giving at a certain level.

● Establish what recognition benefits your donors will receive in return for certain levels of donations and how this will change over time and if donors upgrade their gifts.

● Develop policies by considering different scenarios, circumstances, and types of gifts you receive in your organisation. Try holding a 'brain-storm' with a small group to establish any special considerations that might apply to your organisation.

For example, you may wish to consider:

> ● whether recognition applies to both the donor and his or her spouse.
> ● whether you intend to include gifts-in-kind of the equivalent value.
> ● how you will recognise other gift types; for example, from event participants, pledged gifts (including legacies), or gifts from foundations and corporations.
> ● what periods of time in which gifts, particularly multiple gifts, should be received to qualify for benefits.
> ● how the recognition you provide for your major donors will interface with how you recognise other groups in your organisation: for example, patrons, trustees, ambassadors, and members.
> ● whether gift levels will be inclusive or exclusive of Gift Aid.
> ● how you will publicise your policies, making it clear to donors and staff how gifts will be acknowledged and recognised.

Figure 7.2 relates to criteria for inclusion in membership of the University of Oxford Chancellor's Court of Benefactors.

● Develop a budget for your recognition activities. Doing this in advance will ensure that you are not forced to rush or find less expensive and possibly less than adequate alternatives because of budgetary constraints. For the types of activities you may consider, see the next section in this chapter.

● Develop an implementation framework. Always ensure that the donor wants to be thanked and that you have his or her permission. Consider the following:

> ● What mechanism you will put in place to establish how the donor wishes to be acknowledged and how to seek permission; for example, whether they wish to be listed as Mr and Mrs W Jones, Mr and Mrs William & Susan Jones, or Bill and Sue Jones. Simple ways to ensure that you meet your donors' wishes include adding a section to your pledge card or designing a gift agreement form to

FIGURE 7.2 SAMPLE BENEFACTOR MEMBERSHIP GUIDELINES

University of Oxford: Donor Relations Policy

Guidelines for Membership of the Chancellor's Court of Benefactors

Admission to the Chancellor's Court of Benefactors: An invitation to join the Chancellor's Court of Benefactors may be offered by the Chancellor upon the recommendation of the Pro-Vice-Chancellor (Development & External Affairs) and the General Purposes Committee (GPC), to major benefactors of the University or its Colleges. Membership will be personal to individuals or to representatives of corporations and foundations.

Qualification Level: The normal qualification will be a gift to the Development Programme or a College of at least £1,000,000 from an individual or £2,000,000 from a company, trust or foundation (or the equivalent in another currency).

Individual Donors and Spouses of Individual Donors: Membership of the Court will be for life. The right cannot be inherited but the Pro-Vice-Chancellor (Development & External Affairs) may recommend that upon the death of a major benefactor, in exceptional cases membership should be offered to a member of his/her family. The general presumption applies that, where a gift made jointly by a husband and wife is less than £2,000,000, that gift will attract single membership only. Where a foundation is controlled by the settlor, the gift may be deemed to have come from an individual for the purposes of Court membership.

Corporations and Foundations: Normally the head of the corporation or foundation will be invited to be a member of the Court. Alternatively, although the question of membership will always be explored in the first instance with the head of the corporation or foundation, it may be appropriate for another officer closely involved with the gift to be invited. Membership of the Court will terminate if the individual ceases to hold a relevant post within the corporation or foundation concerned, but it would be open for the Pro-Vice-Chancellor (Development & External Affairs) to invite the corporation or foundation to suggest a successor for the Vice-Chancellor to invite to membership of the Court. The Pro-Vice-Chancellor might also wish, in exceptional cases, to invite members of the Court whose membership would normally terminate to continue to serve for another term. Representation would cease at the same time as a corporation or foundation ceased to function for reasons of bankruptcy, acquisition by another company or the like.

Anonymous Donors: Admission to the Court will be a public act. Anonymous donors who have qualified by the size of their gift should be asked whether they wish to waive their anonymity and accept membership of the Court. It would remain open to the donor to require that the size of the gift should remain confidential.

Gifts to Colleges: An individual donor who has made a gift/gifts to a college totaling £1,000,000 or more, or a company, trust or foundation which has made a gift/gifts totaling £2,000,000 or more, might be invited to become a member of the Court. Heads of House may nominate such donors to be considered for membership of the Court.
[. . .]

allow donors to print their names exactly the way they wish to be recognised, or to mark a box if they want to remain anonymous.

- How and where you will record information relating to recognition activities for individual donors. Establishing a tracking system through your database or in a simple Excel file will help you to monitor and evaluate the effectiveness of your relationship with a donor.

• Evaluate your programme on an annual basis by reviewing how well you achieved your objectives and by seeking feedback from your donors. This could be as simple as telephoning a number of donors to ask them their thoughts. Tweak your programme accordingly.

The London School of Economics uses a gift agreement that is approved by the donor. It includes four headings:

- what the donor has agreed to give
- the use and purpose of the gift
- a schedule for receipt of the gift
- a statement of how the gift will be recognised.

This helps to manage expectations of both the donor and the organisation. On a practical level, it establishes the legal name of the donor and gives the fundraiser the opportunity to discuss how the gift will be recognised or whether the donor wishes to remain anonymous.

Donor Recognition in Practice

Designing a range of recognition activities that are distinctive to your organisation will be the factor that sets your programme apart from others. There is no wrong or right answer. You should establish activities that work for your organisation and that enable you to manage the expectations of those donors seeking recognition.

Consider how you can provide tangible recognition, such as a donor's name on a wall or a plaque, as well as intangible rewards. This might include how you involve and invite feedback from your donors in relation to the work they are funding, or how your donor perceives recognition from and access to senior staff in your organisation.

A distinction between intrinsic rewards (which are central to your mission or work) and extrinsic rewards (which are unrelated) is made by Adrian Sargeant and Elaine Jay in their book, *Building Donor Loyalty*. For example, an intrinsic reward for a donation is a voucher for a meal for two at a restaurant supporting a charity that recycles excess food for the homeless. An example of an extrinsic reward is a pair of tickets to a major tennis tournament, which is unconnected to the work of a homeless charity.

Sargeant and Jay's work on donor loyalty found that donors who were seeking a personal benefit were more likely to lapse as contributors or to be attracted to other causes offering better benefits. The donors who visited the restaurant were more likely to feel connected to the cause by considering how the restaurant makes excess food available to those who need it.

Donor loyalty can therefore be increased if recognition activities are designed around the cause and reinforce the work of the charity in the mind of the donor. The first step is to spend time considering how you can tailor some or all of the following recognition activities so that they underpin the values, ethos, and work of your organisation.

Saying 'Thank You'

The most important component of recognition is the simplest. Saying thank you and providing information about how the gift is to be used are the first steps to building a relationship with your major donor. Consider who, how, and in what form you will thank your donors. See our section in Chapter Six, 'The Art of Thank You'.

FIGURE 7.3 THANK-YOU DRAWING

This drawing by schoolchildren, given in a simple lucite frame, is a cheerful reminder of the positive contribution a donor has made to Andrus Children's Centre, New York.

119

Published Materials

As has been noted above, donors like to see their name alongside others who have given. This can be done either alphabetically or by donation level. Profiling individual donors, their relationships with your organisation, and what motivates them to give can also be a tool to provide appropriate recognition.

Consideration needs to be given to your policy for inclusion and how you will communicate this so that expectations are managed. Consider how you can list or profile your donors in published materials.

- annual report

- newsletter

- updates

- Dedicated donor reports: List all donors in a fundraising calendar year according to different giving levels or alphabetically. This can be used as an insert for a newsletter or as a stand-alone piece.

- Website: Many organisations are turning to the online environment to recognise their supporters. Creating a virtual recognition page offers an inexpensive alternative to donor walls, or reports where lists of donors can be creatively displayed as a way of saying thanks. Profiles can also be used to highlight key donors. Advantages include accessibility, the ability to update or make changes easily, and the opportunity to provide instant feedback and to visibly demonstrate how the gift is being put to work. The main disadvantage is one of confidentiality.

The newsletter from Terrence Higgins Trust for their major donor club, Friends for Life, places their supporters centre stage with photos that reinforce their involvement in the charity. Individual members are listed on the back page and throughout the newsletter there are strong messages of thanks.

The Scripps Research Institute, a biomedical research centre in California, includes on its website a section called 'Recognizing Our Donors'. A number of donors are profiled and each story describes why they have given and how these gifts are making a difference.

City Harvest, a New York based charity that distributes food that would otherwise be wasted, dedicates 50% of its annual report to listing and thanking donors.

FIGURE 7.4 NEWSLETTER FROM TERRENCE HIGGINS TRUST

friends for

life 16

Terrend
HIGGIN
Trus

Dear friends...

...Kindness. That's what's been on my mind recently and in particular, the astonishing kindness that you Friends and Associates show to thousands of people you've never met.

I'm not the only one who has mused about kindness. "The best portion of a good man's life: his little nameless, unremembered acts of kindness and love" was what William Wordsworth had to say on the matter. "Always be kind for everyone is fighting a hard battle" advised Plato. And "Kindness is a golden chain which binds society together" concluded Goethe.

And whilst I'm busy quoting like a busy quotey thing, I can't help mentioning Gladys Browyn Stern who astutely remarked that "Silent gratitude isn't much use to anyone." How right she was, so silent I shall not be. Listen carefully, because I want here and now, loud and clear, to shout my gratitude from the pages of this Newsletter. Thank you. Thank you for your kindness. The vital work of Terrence Higgins Trust would not be possible without you. It's as simple as that. See for yourself: turn over the page... pay them a visit... give them a call – I promise you won't be disappointed.

Now, just as a problem shared is a problem halved – well kindness shared is kindness... well...doubled I suppose – so, as the Americans say, "let's do some math".

Let's get doubling that kindness. Let's give everyone we know the opportunity to feel that wonderful feeling you get from giving. You know the feeling. I mean: the warm glow; the inward smile; the tingly skin; the sweaty palms.

It was Winston Churchill who said, in his wisdom, that "You make a living by what you get. You make a life by what you give." So let's give everyone we know the chance to give; to become a Friend for Life. Go on: rope a chum into my inner circle. I'm getting excited at the mere thought of it! The more the merrier. You can never have too much of a good thing. Many hands make light work. Too many proverbs spoil the broth.

Thank you, dear kind supporters of this wonderful charity of charities. I don't think we can ever say thank you enough.

With love

Stephen Fry
President of Friends for Life

FIGURE 7.5 SCRIPPS WEBSITE DONOR PAGE

TSRI – Giving To Scripps Research

THE
SCRIPPS
RESEARCH
INSTITUTE

Research Advances

Ways to Give

Planning Your Estate

Scripps Research
Champions

Recognizing
Our Donors

Community Health
Education

Conferences,
Lectures & Events

Contact Us

Search

TSRI Home

Give Now

**Subscribe
to E-News**

Philanthropy

Rob and Alison Piziali:
The Promise of Scripps

It's amazing where an idea can take you.

Alison Piziali had the idea that she could make a difference for her young daughter, Tia, and other children afflicted with phenylketonuria (PKU) by raising money to support research in a Scripps Research Institute lab.

After Tia was diagnosed with PKU soon after birth, Alison quickly become aware of the limitations of the current treatment strategy for the disease. Children with PKU–an inherited metabolic disorder—can't convert phenylalanine, a part of a protein, to tyrosine in the liver. Phenylalanine thus becomes toxic to the central nervous system, especially the brain.

Since phenylalanine occurs in meat, fish, all dairy, flour, and even fruits and vegetables, children with PKU must go through life on a severely restricted diet and must be monitored by frequent blood tests. Limiting phenylalanine in the diet is so difficult that many victims fail to avoid behavioral and intellectual problems as adolescents and adults.

Since drug development takes so long, Alison knew she needed to act immediately if she wanted to see new therapeutics available for Tia when she became a teenager.

Alison and her husband Rob Piziali wanted a better fate for their daughter. That's when they learned that Scripps Research Professor Raymond Stevens was working with BioMarin Pharmaceuticals on a potential treatment strategy for PKU and similar diseases. This research showed the promise of using natural cofactors to provide some protection against the toxic effects of phenylalanine for patients with mild PKU and an enzyme replacement strategy for patients with severe PKU.

http://www.scripps.edu/philanthropy/piziali

FIGURE 7.6 ANNUAL REPORT LISTING MAJOR DONORS (CITY HARVEST)

Gifts or Tokens of Appreciation

Off-the-shelf gifts can be boring and add little value to creating a meaningful relationship with your donor, whereas creative approaches stand out. Hand-crafted or unusual gifts that are linked to the mission of your organisation are the most meaningful. With a little creativity, powerful ways of providing recognition can be achieved at little cost.

The NSPCC sent a number of their major donors who have given significantly to their helpline a special 'Box of Memories'. The unique box was filled with hand-crafted quotations and messages from children whose lives had been changed as a result of using the helpline.

Consider the following:

• The type of gift that will reinforce the work of your organisation.

• The type of gift you will give in subsequent years.

• The choice of something that can be displayed in the office or home. This can help to encourage others to give, as well as serve as a constant reminder of the donor's involvement in your organisation.

FIGURE 7.7 'BOX OF MEMORIES' FROM NSPCC

• The actual and the perceived values. Some donors are sensitive to how much money is being spent on them and may not appreciate a gift they perceive to be expensive. The actual value of the benefit must not exceed certain limits in order to qualify for Gift Aid. Table 7.1 illustrates the current regulations, although you should check with HM Revenue & Customs (*http://www.hmrc.gov.uk/charities*) for up-to-date details.

TABLE 7.1 DONOR BENEFITS AND GIFT AID QUALIFICATION

Amount of donation	Value of benefits
£ 0–100	25% of the donation
£ 101–1,000	£25
Above £1,000 donated up to and including 5 April 2007	2.5% of the donation
Above £10,000 donated up to and including 5 April 2007	£250
Above £1,000 donated on or after 6 April 2007	5% of the donation
Above £10,000 donated on or after 6 April 2007	£500

These limits apply separately to each donation. At the time of writing the government was proposing to increase Gift Aid benefit limits from £500 to £2,500 with immediate affect. The previous limit was £500 and applied to donations of more than £10,000. The new limit is likely to apply to donations of more than £50,000. Below that level, a limit of 5 per cent of the donation would apply, the papers show.

The Actors' Fund of America has designed a special paperweight to thank donors who join its Edwin Forrest Society, a major donor club. The gift reinforces the tradition of philanthropy by including a picture of the fund's oldest benefactors as its motif. (See Figure 6.4.)

Awards

Nominating an important donor for an award or medal can be a special way to express your appreciation at very little cost. Some of the most prestigious awards in the UK include:

• The Beacon Fellowship Award, given to individuals who have made exceptional contributions to charitable causes or to organisations that benefit the public.

- Honours awarded by the Queen: these prestigious awards recognise people for all types of service, including teachers, nurses, actors, scientists, diplomats and broadcasters. The largest number of awards go to those providing services to their local communities – mainly volunteers.

- Andrew Carnegie Philanthropy Awards, which recognise some of the world's most prominent philanthropists.

- Marsh Christian Trust presents awards ranging from the Marsh Ecology Award to the Marsh Volunteer of the Year for Work with Children.

- The League of Mercy Awards are given to 50 people each year for voluntary service.

- The Queen's Award for Voluntary Service is for groups that regularly devote their time to helping others in the community.

Some organisations have created their own awards or badges (such as a dedicated coat of arms) as a way of recognising the outstanding philanthropic efforts of their supporters.

FIGURE 7.8 THE SHELDON MEDAL

The University of Oxford developed a new award honouring individual benefactors whose philanthropy has made a significant strategic difference to the University.

The Sheldon Medal, cast in silver, is named after one of Oxford's great early benefactors, Gilbert Sheldon, who as Chancellor (1667–69) funded the construction of the Sheldonian Theatre.

Only two specimens of each medal are produced: a silver presentation piece that is awarded to the donor, and a bronze copy that is displayed in the Ashmolean Museum.

Naming Opportunities

Many organisations have developed permanent recognition displays in the form of plaques or recognition walls. Other naming opportunities include rooms, buildings, chairs, staff positions, events, programmes, and performances. Invest time in planning to ensure that you have a consistent approach.

Considerations

• How easily will the display be updated, with new names added, moved to a different category, or deleted?

• What will be the best place to provide maximum visibility?

• How easily will names be moved around to maintain alphabetical order within categories and at what cost?

• At what point will plaques or names be removed?

• How can you incorporate your mission, story, and photographs into the wall or display to reinforce how these donations make a difference to your end beneficiary?

Consider how you can celebrate the launch or unveiling of the recognition programme by inviting donors to view or unveil a donor wall or plaque.

A site map of adopted woodland

The Trafalgar Woods project by The Woodland Trust gives potential major donor supporters a range of recognition benefits including inclusion in a Roll of Honour and a certificate and site map of the woodland they adopt.

A glittering snowflake for children around the world

The UNICEF Crystal Snowflake is a 16-foot outdoor chandelier designed by Baccarat and lighting designer Ingo Maurer. The snowflake, which is displayed on Fifth Avenue in Manhattan and was lit by the actress Sarah Jessica Parker on the night of the UNICEF Snowflake Ball, displays 16,000 hand-crafted crystals, which are personalised by individuals and corporations who made a donation of $500 or more. In return, each donor receives an exact replica of the engraved crystal to keep as a memento.

An audio-visual display

Glen Falls Hospital in New York installed a digital recognition system with a TV display in a heavily trafficked lobby. The footage includes background on the hospital's campaign, a scrolling list of donors by category (easily updated by web-based content management systems), and the history of the hospital and campaign.

A permanent tribute in the heart of the community

The Log House Museum is a small museum that celebrates the founding of Seattle, Washington. The Founders' Circle is a granite and marble piece recognising individuals, businesses, and agencies that are major donors to the museum. The circle, which was inspired by a design from a tribe whose heritage is linked to Seattle, was unveiled at a special dedication ceremony on the anniversary of the landing of a famous settler. A special new blend of coffee was developed – Seattle is the home of the Starbucks coffee chain – and each major donor was given a bag of it as an expression of thanks.

Special access
Providing access to private parts of your museum or new building or enabling your senior and operational staff to meet with your donors signal clearly to them that you consider their support and involvement to be important. Finding opportunities to involve them or to seek their advice about the future of your organisation or project provides recognition and respect for their intellectual and business achievements. Meeting with your operational staff allows them to hear first-hand from the people closest to your cause and to see their passion.

City Harvest, a charity in New York City that recycles food for the homeless that would otherwise be wasted, offers a ride in a delivery truck as a way of thanking and engaging donors in its work.

Each board meeting at the Crohn's and Colitis Foundation in New York City is held at a different location. Before each meeting, a dinner is held, and major donors living locally are invited to meet the organisation's leadership. The dinners form an effective way of thanking donors in different parts of the country and recognising the contributions they make.

Consider how you can facilitate this type of access in your ordinary calendar of activities to deepen the commitment of your donors and their understanding of your work.

Recognition Events

Events are widely used by organisations as a mechanism to cultivate or to secure repeat gifts as part of a giving society or club. They are also used to recognise formally the support of individual donors or collective members of a society or club. Events are most effective when they work to establish a stronger relationship between your donors and your organisation. You should ensure that you find a way of including educational programmes. Organising events in the same time period each year helps donors schedule their plans.

Events offer the opportunity to provide face-to-face recognition and information about the cause. The challenge is to ensure that these events do not become repetitive and boring but instead retain a specific purpose, create an appropriate ambiance, and demonstrate the gift at work.

Many fundraisers agree that, even if the donor isn't able to attend, receiving an invitation to an event provides a small way of increasing involvement and engagement.

Recognition Societies

A patron or high-level-giving club is a programme of activity designed to facilitate annual gifts at predetermined levels. Gift clubs provide a mechanism for acknowledging, publicising, and celebrating donors who make a continuing commitment to your cause. Gift clubs are increasingly used as a mechanism to drive regular high-value giving. Gift sizes range enormously, but most gift clubs have an entry level of a minimum annual donation of £1,000, followed by a tiered number of gifts, e.g. £5,000, £10,000, and £50,000. As part of their membership, donors receive certain benefits, and these privileges increase with the size of the donation. Many gift clubs are headed by a patron, who is often a high-profile individual and who hosts events associated with the club.

For some organisations (particularly those in the arts, where there is more opportunity to provide a range of desirable benefits through access to exhibitions, and in education, where there is a predefined community in the alumni), recognition societies have proven to be highly effective in generating new income.

Successful giving clubs have something distinctive to offer, either through benefits, such as access to special programmes, exhibitions, or privileged information, or through association with high-profile individual supporters. The most effective programmes have a marketing strategy, which creates a sense of belonging and a 'community' of club members making a difference, through functions, events, and donor communications.

The use of benefits as an incentive to giving has prompted some debate. As we have seen earlier, donors who are motivated by rewards are more likely to lapse as continuing contributors than other types of donors. What seems more likely is that these rewards-oriented donors are already predisposed to giving to the organisation and that the club provides them with an opportunity to give. The donor recognition component of the club is therefore secondary to the belief in the organisation.

Establishing a gift club has the advantage of:

• developing a prospect pool for significant gifts.

• providing an ascending ladder of levels to encourage 'upgrades' and motivate donors to increase their commitments.

• raising unrestricted income, as most gift clubs are not associated with a particular programme of activity but the work of the charity in general.

• providing predictable and dependable income, once the club is established.

• providing a structured way of engaging a group of individuals in your work through an organised programme of activities.

• generating the impetus for major-gift fundraising in an organisation with high-level friends who haven't yet given.

• creating a sense of belonging and permanence. When people see that their friends, colleagues, or peers think that an organisation is important enough to support, it encourages them to do the same.

• establishing benchmarks for giving to your organisation.

• implying or offering status, particularly at higher giving levels, as clubs provide an opportunity to be part of a group that not everyone can join.

Gift clubs need to be introduced with care. Many fail because they have not:

• been thoroughly costed out (expenses from staff time to stationery can have a big impact on your budget).

• been monitored for effectiveness.

• considered factors such as how the programme affects stakeholders in your organisation, e.g. existing donors, patrons, trustees, or members.

If the club exhibits the same levels of loyalty and value of average donors over time, the scheme should be reconsidered. Common mistakes include continuing out of inertia, rather than regularly reviewing effectiveness and valuing these donors more highly than others, when in fact others may be more valuable.

Consider the following:

• A major gift club may restrict or cap your organisation's ability to generate gifts of substance that are achieved only through personal solicitation and cultivation.

• A gift club can become a 'mass marketing' transaction-based activity at odds with relationship fundraising.

• A club requires a long-term commitment.

• Initially, you are likely to see a drop in income from your direct-mail solicitations as donors move from one programme to the other.

Design considerations for a major gift club

Here we outline some of the key steps to consider when developing a plan for a recognition club for your organisation.

Staffing the programme. How will the programme be resourced? Will new staff be needed to research and cultivate new members and to ask them to join? Keep in mind the support you will need from other staff in operations or development when deciding on structure and benefits – it is better to under-promise and over-deliver.

Creating an identity. A distinctive, identifiable entity to include a name, logo, and identity. Consider the following ideas:

• Choose a name with longevity. Don't be topical or programme-specific, because this could change with time.

• Establish an umbrella name with subgroups that are distinctive in their own right; e.g. City Harvest: Harvesters, Growers, Sowers, Gleaners.

• Name the club after a founder or individual who has played a significant role in your organisation; e.g. the Edwin Forrest Society.

• Approach a celebrity to head the club, therefore implying status.

• Develop a distinctive identity including stationery and logo.

Servicing the club. The most successful method of recruiting new donors is through face-to-face solicitation. New prospects and club members require firstclass service, including hand-addressed and signed letters. At an annual dinner, ensure the meal is as fine as possible. Consider ways in which you can involve members, making them feel part of the 'inner circle' of your organisation.

Selecting appropriate member benefits. Decide on appropriate gift levels for your organisation. This will be dependent upon factors that are specific to your institution, such as average gift size, number of gifts received at a specified level, and number of prospective members at each level. As a rule of thumb, you should ensure that you have a history of receiving one or more donations at the top end of the scale. You can always add new levels later. The most common levels are:

• £1,000–£2,499
• £2,500–£4,999
• £5,000–£9,999
• £10,000–£24,999
• £25,000 or more.

Choose benefits that bring your donors into the fold and make them feel more engaged with the organisation and what it does: develop intrinsic rewards.

- A ride in the truck that delivers meals to the homeless
- A nature tour with one of your conservationist for a nature charity
- Use of a dedicated coat of arms
- A piece of clothing made from the founder's family tartan
- Lunch with the scientist or outreach worker being funded
- Access to trustees at a dinner for a rotating board meeting.

Develop a marketing strategy that underpins your brand values but that implies exclusivity, status, and the expectation of special privileges and treatment.

- Don't overcomplicate the programme: keep it simple. While structure and identity are important, the success of your programme will be based on donor relationships.

- You should be able to remember easily the details of the levels and benefits (if you don't, your major donor won't).

- Establish rules of eligibility. (See the section earlier in this chapter on recognition policy development.)

- Underpin your programme with an emphasis on making personal relationships with your donors whenever possible.

- Inform those who already give at that level, share the exciting new programme, and consider how you might recognise their continuing commitment.

- Personalise letters.

- Determine how this giving circle fits with your other high-level groups, such as existing donors, celebrity patrons, trustees, members, and foundation and corporate donors.

> The Chancellor's Court of Benefactors is a major gift club at Oxford University. Members are invited to join and receive privileges such as attendance at the Chancellor's lunch. They are also entitled to wear the distinctive robes and bonnet of the Court.

The following examples of major gift clubs illustrate the types of benefits offered to members.

FIGURE 7.9   THE ASIA SOCIETY'S CHAIRMAN'S CIRCLE

Chairman's Circle

The Chairman's Circle is the highest-level donor group at the Asia Society. Its members will be recognized in print and with invitations to special events. In addition, they will have ready access to the Chairman of the Society's Board of Trustees and he will consult with them regularly on questions of importance to the future of the Society.

K. Rupert Murdoch, Chairman and CEO of News Corporation Limited, with former U.S. Secretary of State Henry Kissinger.

Benefactor ($25,000 and above)

- Opportunity to host private dinners with Asia Society Chairman
- Consultation with Asia Society curators on collecting Asian art (by request)
- Guidance and advice on travel to Asia
- Assistance with facilitating introductions to Asian art, policy and business dignitaries

and all benefits listed below

Sponsor ($10,000)

- Private meeting with Asia Society Chairman, Richard C. Holbrooke (by request)
- Private curator-led tour of the museum for ten guests while musuem is closed to the public (by request)
- Special behind-the-scenes tour of Asia Society Museum vault with curator
- Invitations to:
  - VIP exhibition opening dinners
  - All private collection and artist studio visits
- Complimentary registration for two to the Society's Annual Corporate Conference in Asia
- Complimentary admission for two to all public programs with prior registration
- Copies of all Asia Society exhibition catalogues
- A one-year Contributing Individual gift membership ($250 value)

General Pervez Musharraf, President of Pakistan, speaking at a Policy luncheon entitled "New Architecture for Peace and Stability in South Asia.

Above: Prime Minister of the Kingdom of Thailand, Dr. Thaksin Shinawatra, walking with Maurice R. Greenberg, Chairman and CEO of American International Group, Inc. and Asia Society Chairman Emeritus and trustee, and Nicholas Platt, Asia Society President.
Right: Visual Artist Shahzia Sikander and Salman Khokhar with Vishakha Desai, Asia Society Senior Vice President and Director of the Museum and Cultural programs, and Robert B. Oxnam, Asia Society President Emeritus.

Additional Benefits

Chairman's Circle members receive all benefits available to members of the President's Circle and Friends of Asian Arts. These include:

- Dinner with Asia Society President Nicholas Platt or Asia Society Museum Director, Vishakha N. Desai (by request)
- Invitations to:
  - VIP dinners with Asian art, policy and business leaders
  - Intimate, privately-hosted dinners with special guests
  - Exhibition previews and private, curator-led tours
  - Asia Society Caravan, which visits unusual and exclusive sites in Asia
- Copies of all Asian Update publications and Archives of Asian Art journals
- Complimentary audio transcripts of Society programs (by request)
- Priority seating at select performing arts and public programs
- Unlimited free admission to the Asia Society Museum
- Discounts on admission to all performances, films, lectures and symposia, purchases in AsiaStore, and Garden Court Café

The Dalai Lama at an Asia Society President's Forum.

132

FIGURE 7.10 CancerBACKUP BENEFACTOR PROGRAMME

FIGURE 7.11 ACTIONAID AMBASSADOR'S PLEDGE CARD

Pledge card

I / We would like to join the ActionAid Ambassador Network ☐

I / We would like to make a donation of

£25,000 ☐   £20,000 ☐   £10,000 ☐   £5,000 ☐

Other amount please state   £...................................

Date by which donation will be paid ....

giftaid it ☐ Please send me a Gift Aid declaration form

Name...
Address..
Postcode.......................... Email...
Tel..Mobile.......................................
Signed..Date..................................

ActionAid would like to thank you for your generous support

ActionAid is a registered charity No. 274467

133

FIGURE 7.12 THE BRITISH HEART FOUNDATION'S HEART PIONEERS' INVITATION LETTER

British Heart Foundation

Mr A B Sample
1 Sample Street
Sample Town
Sample County
XX1 1XX

14 Fitzhardinge Street
London
W1H 6DH

t• 020 7935 0185
f• 020 7486 5820
w• bhf.org.uk

May 2004

Dear Mr Sample

Your name has been passed to me as someone who might consider being part of a select group of people. These people are called Heart Pioneers because, quite simply, they are the very heart of our pioneering research.

As you may know, the British Heart Foundation has been behind many of the significant successes in the fight against heart disease. We currently support over 30 world-leading professors conducting pioneering research.

I was a Professor in Southampton long before I became Medical Director of the British Heart Foundation. I know first-hand the difference the support of the British Heart Foundation makes. Research takes time, effort, determination, and a considerable amount of patience - all towards the goal of saving lives. I thought it a shame that more people don't get to experience how fantastic a research scientist's 'eureka!' moments can be.

[...]

I'll leave the rest for Professor Deanfield to explain at the first Heart Pioneers meeting during British Heart Week on Monday 7th June. Need I say that this date is not far off.

You will find everything you need to become 1 in 100 enclosed. It is a pioneering venture, in true British Heart Foundation spirit. It's also a unique way of seeing just how much of a difference you are making, right at our heart.

Sincerely,

Professor Sir Charles George BSc MD FRCP
Medical Director, British Heart Foundation

FIGURE 7.13 THE LIBERTY PARTNERSHIP PROGRAMME FROM THE
FOOD BANK FOR NEW YORK CITY

LIBERTY PARTNERSHIP
FREEDOM *from* HUNGER

October 22, 2003

Dear Sample A. Sample,

The tragedy faced by 1.5 million New Yorkers is often ignored -- but not by you.

As a loyal supporter of the Food Bank you understand that so many are deprived of the most basic necessity. And that they are little children ... hardworking parents ... struggling retirees -- all in need of food assistance.

In recognition of your compassion for our less fortunate neighbors -- *and your generosity as a donor* -- the Food Bank For New York City invites you to play an <u>even more vital role</u>.

By annually making a gift of $1,000 or more[*], you will become part of an extraordinary circle of New Yorkers -- Food Bank's ***Liberty Partnership.***

Liberty Partners are concerned neighbors who know that the Food Bank is the <u>one</u> organization that can handle the enormity of our ongoing hunger crisis. And they are committed to joining us as <u>leaders</u> in this fight.

In recognition of your exceptional commitment, we are offering you special ***Liberty Partnership, Freedom From Hunger*** benefits. Please see the enclosed brochure for details on these rewarding opportunities.

Together, we can be a powerful force for creating change and hope for those who are hungry in this great city. Won't you extend your generosity once more and become a ***Liberty Partner*** today?

Warmly,

Lucy Cabrera

Lucy Cabrera, Ph.D.
President & CEO

P.S.   We continue to face great challenges and your ongoing support is more vital than ever. Last year, we supplied enough food to help provide more than 200,000 meals a day. As a ***Liberty Partner***, you'll enable us to accomplish even more in these difficult times.

*Our fiscal year is July 2003 through June 2004.

Food Bank For New York City
Hunts Point Cooperative Market • 355 Food Center Drive • Bronx, New York 10474-7515

135

You should ask the following key questions regarding each major donor. If you ask, answer, and act on these, you will be best-placed to ensure that you are meeting donor expectations and managing relationships according to your donors' wishes.

TABLE 7.2 CHECKLIST FOR MANAGING MAJOR DONORS

1. What type of contact should we be making and how frequently should we make it?	Letters, phone calls, e-mails, progress reports, invitations to events (both donor-specific and as part of the charity's programme) should all be considered and identified.
2. Are we treating this donor with the respect he or she deserves and expects?	On receipt of a major donation, have we written immediately to thank the donor with a personal letter? Have we ensured that either the chairman or the chief executive (in addition to or rather than the fundraiser) has written the letter?
3. Are we timing our requests appropriately?	Have we guarded against placing this donor's name on a mailing list or other kind of mechanism that insults him or her by asking for another donation hard on the heels of receipt of a major cheque?
4. Do we know from first-hand experience how committed the donor is to our particular charity and how actively involved with the work of the charity he or she wishes to become?	If so, what personal plan have we developed that could help the donor get closer to the organisation and how has this been communicated?
5. Do we know if the donor is in a position to offer professional skills?	What are they, can we use them, and how have we responded to this?
6. How much public recognition do donors want and in what form?	Have we offered anything public? Should we? What kinds of recognition would be appropriate for this person?
7. Who in the organisation and what aspects of the charity's work would the donor like to meet or experience?	What are we arranging to meet this need?

Reproduced from *Building Relationships with Donors*, Institute of Philanthropy & Ansbacher Group 2003

Conclusion

Recognition is an essential component of effective donor stewardship. Spending time developing appropriate policies and planning appropriate and distinctive recognition activities will help to ensure that you meet and exceed the expectations of your donors. In doing so, you will be in a position to build trust, loyalty, and commitment from your donors, solidifying their support for the longer term.

References

Breeze, Beth, *The Coutts Million Pound Donor Report*, 2009

Lloyd, T, *Why Rich People Give*. Association of Charitable Foundations, 2004.

Prince, R and File, K, *The Seven Faces of Philanthropy*. Jossey-Bass, 1994.

Sargeant, A and Jay, E, *Building Donor Loyalty*. Jossey-Bass, 2004.

Lannon, J, *Managing Major Donors*. Institute of Philanthropy & the Ansbacher Group, 2003.

Talking about results, New Philanthropy Capital, 2010

CHAPTER EIGHT

Creating a Major Donor Programme Culture: How to Get Your Board and Staff Ready

Teamwork is the ability to work together toward a common vision. It is the ability to direct individual accomplishments toward organizational objectives and is the fuel that allows common people to attain uncommon results.
— *Andrew Carneige*

What you'll learn in this chapter

- The importance of collaborative fundraising
- How to motivate your board members to become involved
- How to incorporate fundraising throughout your organisation.

Introduction

Major gift fundraising should not be a solitary effort. Rather, it is the culmination of a collective effort across the organisation to create a major donor-friendly culture within your charity. This is where teamwork and collaboration between the fundraiser and the volunteer leadership is critical. American charities long ago realised the importance of this partnership. Most now stress the fundraising role of the board to prospective board members, refusing to add new members to the board who are unwilling to assist in the process. They also involve their professional staff, such as programme directors and heads of departments where appropriate. There are many ways they can help in each of the three stages of major gift solicitations. Now that you have a thorough understanding of the techniques and processes involved in major gift fundraising, this chapter brings us full-circle to the place where you need to begin. This chapter will help you create an across-the-organisation major gift programme.

Developing a Major Gifts Culture in Your Organisation

Creating a culture that permeates your organisation and recognises the continual intense efforts to implement and manage a successful major gift programme requires patience, fortitude, and an enthusiastic, proactive leader, whether it is your CEO or board chairman, or another influential volunteer leader. Equally important is to create an understanding of the importance of fundraising with your programme staff, as they too can be great fundraising ambassadors for your charity.

How do you develop the culture in your organisation that encourages the building of a successful major gift programme? We suggest that you begin by communicating your fundraising progress to the rest of the staff. For example, SeeAbility, a 200-year-old charity that has worked with people who are blind or partially sighted and have additional disabilities such as physical and learning disabilities, degenerative illnesses, brain injuries, and mental health problems, had a prospect who was the chairman of a major insurance company and who was close to SeeAbility's national office and interested in its work. SeeAbility's volunteer coordinator invited the prospect to a training day on visual impairment and then to accompany groups of visually impaired people on an outing. This experience was the turning point for the prospect, who committed to a £65,000 donation. The funding team made a point of calling the volunteer coordinator to share the good news and to recognise the part she had played in the successful solicitation.

So, where possible, involve your programme and operations staff in developing proposals for prospects and meeting with your major gift donors and prospects. The staff at a major American cancer hospice telephoned the major-donor officer to tell him that a high-profile celebrity had stopped by to drop off several boxes of toys his children no longer used. Tipping off the major-donor staff meant they could follow up with this prospect in the most appropriate way with the idea of building a longer-term relationship. The fundraising team was so appreciative that they sent the hospice staff a cake to express their thanks. Many American charities ask their programme officers, when they are travelling on business or attending a conference, to telephone donors in that area and thank them for their gifts or to have breakfast or lunch with the donor.

Communicating regularly with your colleagues, your boss, and your volunteer leadership may be the most effective way to build the major-donor-focused culture in your organisation. Quarterly e-mail updates, reports at weekly or monthly staff meetings, or reports at board meetings are some of the effective ways to help educate staff and volunteers about the importance of major gift work. You may also want to make a presentation during other team meetings, outlining what cultivation means and the roles that everyone in the organisation plays to help build relationships with donors.

'We had a fundraising day where we educated the wider organisation about the roles, practices, and functions of major gift fundraising.'
– Friends of the Earth

139

Many organisations are now investing in formal training for major gift fundraising to create a supportive culture.

> 'To help educate our people on the inside, we organised internal training specifically on major donor fundraising. About one third of the organisation (75 people) received this training which was delivered by an external consultant in a one-day programme. Every senior manager received the training right across the organisation, from the Celebrity Manager, the Director of Scotland to the Regional Area Managers. We did this so that they understand how it works. We're exposing major donors to staff across the organisation and if they can understand how it works then they can see how they can play a role in inspiring major donors. The whole organisation is involved in the programme.'
>
> – The Woodland Trust

We also encourage you to begin working with one or two trustees to develop criteria for adding fundraising-savvy trustees to your board or to establish a separate fundraising committee, or both.

This brings us to the roles of the senior staff, volunteers, and board of trustees in any successful major gift programme.

Fundraising Staff and Key Volunteer Roles for a Successful Major Gift Programme

Though some groups have relied on a celebrity or one person with local name recognition to start a major gift programme, the most effective programmes have developed roles for each member of the charity's fundraising team: the board, board committees, other key leadership volunteers, chief executive officer, programme staff, chief fundraising officer, major gifts officer, and the remainder of the fundraising staff.

The Board and Trustees

Let's begin with the fundamental principle of developing a committed board. The board sets the tone for fundraising. By virtue of their nomination or appointment to your charity's board, they are individuals who bring expertise in varied fields, are truly interested in and supportive of your charity's mission, are often highly respected, and have wide personal and professional networks. In the best of all possible worlds, they should also be influential people at the pinnacle of their professional or volunteer lives who will make the best ambassadors for your charity's mission. It is important to remember that not all of them will be practised or even willing fundraisers.

The best charity boards are a diverse group of individuals with different skill sets: those with a financial background who take seriously their role to ensure the fiscal stability of the charity; some with programme knowledge that comes from being either a recipient of your organisation's services (e.g. an alumnus or a patient) or an expert in the field of your charity's work; several with excellent networks to enable your charity to influence action; and several who are unafraid to ask for gifts. Ideally, a charity board would have as many as 60% of the trustees willing to assist the organisation in actively raising funds. But such a situation is usually extraordinary; more likely, we find boards with a very small percentage of eager fundraisers.

'My chairman, Deian Hopkin, is fearless,' said Alistair Lomax, Executive Director of UNIAID. 'We prepared a list of prospective donors for the board's review and he ticked over 200 names, wrote personally to each of them, and opened so many doors for us.' It's not difficult to get involvement like this. But it needs to be established as part of the induction process. It is at this point that we are best able to support new colleagues and give them a sense of clarity and confidence about the role they can each play in the fundraising process.

In fact, not everyone is cut out to be a fearless fundraiser, says Simon Sperryn, CEO of Lloyd's Market Association, the former head of the London Chamber of Commerce and board member of UNIAID, a UK charity whose aim is to help students cope with financial hurdles to higher education. 'The personal qualities needed to make a successful *ask* are unusual, and I hugely respect those who can do it', he says. Among the qualities Mr Sperryn cites for successful trustee fundraisers are:

- a degree of confidence

- a belief in the cause of the charity

- a personal connection to the charity, tempered by a professional objectivity.

Mr Sperryn also maintains that boards need members with a range of skills and perceptions around the table, keeping in mind that not everyone will be able to assist with fundraising.

'However we found important common ground in three respects: (a) that trustees have an inescapable duty to ensure that the charity is financially sustainable, and therefore funding is a number one concern for them; (b) that even those who are not well placed to raise funds may be surprised how much they have to offer, for example by making their contacts or their name available; and (c) that their role in fundraising, if any, should not be taken for granted or assumed but addressed before their appointment and confirmed in the letter of appointment.'

What should you do if this is your situation? Don't wistfully dream that all of your board members will either resign or suddenly see the fundraising light. Instead, plan to recruit new members as the nucleus of a new board which understands its role in the fundraising process. Be clear about your organisation's need to have a board that not only gives personally significant gifts, but that also helps the professional staff identify, cultivate, solicit, and be a steward for prospects and donors. 'Trustees should be told before they start that one of the trustees' primary responsibilities is to make sure the charity is being funded,' Mr Sperryn says, 'whether that is from personal contributions by the trustees, a willingness to help with introductions and asking, or making sure the staff is successfully raising funds.'

Enlisting board members who will make a difference is crucial to the success of any major gift programme. It is vitally important that the members of the fundraising team are included in the nominating process, and that nominees are asked a series of questions that allow the person to define what she or he expects to bring to the organisation. For instance,

• Every board operates somewhat differently. If you were asked to join this board, what do you think your responsibilities would include?

• What would you bring to this board?

Make sure your questions are clearly understood, and when you refer to a major gift, define what it means to your charity. Be sure to test the prospective member's understanding of your charity's mission and philanthropy by using the following questions:

• What does [your charity's name] mean to you?

• How would you go about the task of bringing in £5,000 as a member of this board?

Some American charities have gone so far as to ask trustees to adopt a board resolution that clearly states the role of trustees in the fundraising programme, similar to the one that the American Kidney Fund adopted in 1998. (See the *Sample Documents* section at the end of this chapter.)

However, to expect all board members to understand the importance of fundraising and major gifts without giving them any training is a mistake. Every new board member should receive training in how to present essential facts of the charity's mission and programmes and how to ask for gifts effectively, and should be assigned an experienced board member as a mentor. They should also be given a job assignment that matches their particular interest, is not too arduous, and is carried out with other board members.

> 'We've used consultants to present a half-day major-donor training to members of our Executive Appeal Team. We then produced a mini-guide that is a printed 'quick reference' for the team members to have with them before a meeting. It's a way of thinking about our most important donors' needs and making the task we're asking the team members to do a bit easier. The training really helped build a culture supportive of major donor fundraising and improved their under-standing of major-gift fundraising and added to their confidence.'
>
> – The Healing Foundation

Caveat. Do not expect your board to change overnight. Changing the responsibilities of trustees typically takes a considerable period of time. It may take several generations of boards before the majority of the trustees understand, personally support, and actively raise funds for your organ-isation. Your goal should be to get one new trustee with fundraising experience in each year's nomination process. For instance, if your board members' terms of office are three years and you have 15 trustees, with three of them rotating off the board annually, it could take as many as nine cycles to reach the goal of 60% of the board being willing fundraisers.

The Fundraising Committee

Once you have a cadre of board members who are experienced, passionate, and willing to raise money, you should consider developing a fundraising committee. Or if you can't get your board to embrace fundraising, you may need to develop an alternative method of involving volunteer leaders by establishing a fundraising committee. The purpose of this committee is to oversee and advise the organisation's fundraising activities. Its main duties are to:

• set policies, priorities, and goals for fundraising programmes for the current fiscal year

• review the performance of each campaign

• review campaign achievements versus objectives

• identify and rate all major prospects for support

• recruit key volunteer leadership and fundraisers for the organisation's campaigns

• act as ambassadors to assist the fundraising office in identification, cultivation, solicitation, and stewardship of prospects and donors.

This committee should have equal status with the other important board committees, such as finance and investment, nominations, and pro-grammes. A chairman or chairwoman should be selected to lead the efforts in a partnership with the professional fundraising staff to identify, cultivate, and solicit, and provide stewardship for prospects and donors. A sample job description for a fundraising committee chairmanship is in the *Resource* section at the end of this chapter.

One organisation, SeeAbility, has developed a special group of indi-viduals who are called Ambassadors to assist with its major gifts campaign. Functioning much like a fundraising committee, the roles and responsi-bilities of both the Ambassadors and the SeeAbility staff are clearly outlined and include:

• publicly endorsing the goals of the charity
• facilitating support from companies, individuals, and trusts
• making a personal contribution
• advising on strategic, campaign, and other planning issues to ensure the success of the fundraising efforts.

Royal Patrons, Vice Presidents and Ambassadors can be valuable to the major gift fundraising programme, especially if they are high-profile. While they may not always be prepared to give financial support (although this should always be the goal), they may be more willing to lend their support as figureheads by hosting events such as pledge dinners or attending recep-tions. This can be a valuable way of encouraging donors to attend. If you don't have any high-profile supporters, use your prospect research skills developed in Chapter Three to identify individuals who have an interest in your cause.

Chief Executive Officer

The chief executive officer is the 'face of the charity' to those outside the organisation. The CEO is most often the charity's spokesman and has the closest ties to the trustees and extensive insider knowledge about the charity. For this reason, CEOs typically are the most effective fundraisers. We have found that many non-profit CEOs would rather visit the dentist for a root canal than participate actively in fundraising. Often caught up in the day-to-day administration of their organisations, CEOs frequently say they don't have time to devote to fundraising or they insist that it is the job of the fundraiser to raise the money. Conversely, some profess deep immersion in fundraising, but in fact they are minimally involved.

Substantial involvement by the CEO is a critical step in developing a successful major gift programme. Individuals who are capable and willing to make transformative gifts want to have access to those in positions of leadership and in many cases need to receive personalised attention at a level that only the CEO can give.

> 'Our CEO is very involved and our chairman has significant networks. Our chairman will often raise a potential new contact with our CEO. Our CEO likes to make the initial phone call to approach the prospect and will invite them in for a meeting.'
>
> – CancerBACKUP

CEOs of American charities must have fundraising experience. With the profusion of charities in the United States today (more than 900,000 and growing), the rivalry for donors is extraordinarily intense; therefore, many non-profits have recruited senior development officers to become CEOs. The job description for the president/CEO of the Advocacy Institute (see the *Sample Documents* section at the end of this chapter) is a good example of the priority that American charities place on this level of commitment by the CEO. Several British charities are beginning to recruit CEOs actively to assist the fundraising process.

Major Gifts Officer or Chief Fundraiser

Along with shouldering the primary responsibility of raising money from a select group of high-net-worth individuals, the role of the major gifts officer (MGO) is to be the advocate for the major gifts programme within the organisation. Often, the MGO finds himself or herself competing with other members of the fundraising team for access to donors or prospects. For instance, if a patron of a special event is capable of making another large gift outright, occasionally the fundraiser who is charged with managing the special event will be reluctant to allow access to the donor, fearing that the donor will be overwhelmed and stop supporting the organisation altogether. Understanding that the closer the relationship to the charity the donor has the more interested he or she will become in the organisation, and therefore the more likely to make a significant investment in its future, is an important thing for staff to realise. We call this seeing the individual in 360 degrees – in this case – not just as an event chair but as a potential major donor as well.

Raising significant sums from individuals, as we noted in Chapter Two, takes an enormous amount of time, and this can try the patience of the CEO as well as the fundraising committee and ultimately the trustees. The major gifts officer must have well-developed diplomacy skills, a solid belief in the process, and the ability to explain the importance of the long-term investment to colleagues, his or her boss, and the volunteer leadership.

The typical American major gifts officer reports to the senior fundraiser, with whom he or she works closely to develop and implement the major gifts programme. MGOs usually have five or more years of experience in a fundraising office, an aptitude for clear thinking, extremely well-honed speaking and writing skills, a prodigious memory, a mastery of etiquette, and a deep devotion to the charity's mission, and are personable, interesting people. In short, such an MGO is someone you would like to have dinner with or spend five days with on an overseas trip seeing the results of your charity's work.

Because this work is so intense and detail-oriented, major gifts officers should handle a donor portfolio of only 120 to 200 individuals. They must keep detailed records of donor contacts, and be able to map out effectively a series of steps leading either to closing a gift or upgrading a donor to a higher level of giving. A typical job description for a major gifts officer in an American charity can be found in the *Sample Documents* section at the end of this chapter. Note the requirements of training volunteers to be better 'askers' and working closely with their programming colleagues.

Conclusion

We cannot emphasise strongly enough the importance of establishing a thriving major-donor culture within your organisation. For without it and clearly defined roles for the essential partners in the major gifts programme, charities find themselves doing more harm than good with their donors. Gradually developing either a fundraising board, or a fully functioning advisory committee or fundraising committee, is an important step. Working closely with your CEO to develop and implement the programme, and finally working on an equal footing with your programme colleagues, should help guarantee your success.

Sample Documents

Resolution,
Board of Trustees,
American Kidney Fund, May 16, 1998

Whereas the board of trustees of American Kidney Fund, Inc. (AKF) acknowledges that, as a not-for-profit corporation, a primary source of organisational income is from fundraising, and the future growth and success of our organisation relates directly to the success of fundraising efforts, and success in fundraising is directly dependent upon our ability to cultivate and solicit large-gift donors, and prospective individual, corporate and foundation large-gift donors will be more receptive to solicitation knowing that the board of trustees are actively involved in giving of their own personal resources and in the cultivation and asking processes.

Now therefore, the board of trustees does hereby resolve to adopt job descriptions for trustees and committee members which include the following:

• It is board policy that each trustee contributes financially to the organisation each year to the very best of his or her ability.

• Trustees recognise that fundraising is the lifeblood of the organisation and that leadership is set by example. Each trustee agrees to participate in the cultivation and asking processes on an ongoing basis.

Job Description: President/CEO,
The Advocacy Institute, Washington, DC

Job summary
The Advocacy Institute seeks a President/CEO to lead this highly regarded Washington-based non-profit institution. Since its founding 20 years ago, the Advocacy Institute has played a major role in developing and strengthening the leaders of organisations devoted to social and economic justice in this country and around the world.

This is an exceptional opportunity to shape, challenge and inspire a new generation of public interest leaders. The position requires a person with a passion for the organisation's mission and core values, a creative intellect, an entrepreneurial temperament and a history of hands-on involvement in and dedication to social and economic justice. The Institute currently has a budget of $5 million and a staff of eighteen.

About The Advocacy Institute

The Advocacy Institute's extraordinary work involves finding gifted social justice advocates in the United States and around the world and strengthening their skills, broadening their networks, deepening their effectiveness, and sustaining their efforts. The Advocacy Institute has worked with more than 2,500 non-profit organisations in 62 countries and has inspired thousands of social justice advocates worldwide. Its work has been translated into a dozen languages, most recently Arabic.

The Advocacy Institute has used many formats to meet the needs of social justice advocates. It provides tools and learning environments that are customised to reflect the needs of the individual leader's situation and organisation. The goal is to create both immediate and long-term improvements in the way advocacy leaders approach their work. The Advocacy Institute has two broad programmatic areas: the Advocacy Leaders Program and Leadership for a Changing World.

The Advocacy Leaders Program designs and conducts domestic and international advocacy leadership development programmes, based on extensive needs assessments. These programmes engage social justice advocates, enhance their advocacy skills, connect them within and across issue sectors and provide them with strategic guidance and support.

In 2001, the Advocacy Institute was selected by the Ford Foundation to design and implement the Leadership for a Changing World programme because of its longstanding experience with identifying and supporting emerging community leaders with diverse interests and backgrounds. Leadership for a Changing World, in partnership with the Ford Foundation and the Robert F Wagner Graduate School of Public Service at New York University, was created to recognise extraordinary leaders working to improve lives in communities all across the United States.

About the President/CEO position

In conjunction with the Board of Trustees, staff, programme alumni and other stakeholders, the President/CEO will develop a vision and action plan to guarantee that AI will continue to play a vital role in developing new advocacy leaders. The strategy and vision should go beyond current activities and lay out the means by which AI can become a more active catalyst for change.

• Develop and implement a strategy for a comprehensive fundraising programme that is aligned with the organisation's vision and provides support for programmes in the near and long term.

• Actively pursue and secure new diverse sources of revenue from major donors and foundations, as well as from its products and services; engage the Board in fundraising activities as appropriate.

• Create a strong working relationship with the Board, ensuring that its members are appropriately informed of current and emerging issues and are judiciously called upon for their expertise and consultation. In addition, act as a catalyst to strengthen the Board in all aspects of its work.

• Seize opportunities for advancing and supporting effective advocacy work through thoughtful attention to the changing needs of communities, emerging political developments and the challenges and opportunities presented by new technology.

• Ensure that staff, Board members and programme participants are diverse and representative of the complexity of the larger society.

• Create strategic alliances with other organisations that have complementary interests and missions.

• Provide cohesive internal management to ensure that the Advocacy Institute can meet its goals and objectives.

• Manage financial and internal compliance systems so that the organisation and its leadership can readily fulfill their legal and fiduciary responsibilities.

• Strengthen and develop the Advocacy Institute programmes that support advocacy leaders globally.

• Serve as spokesperson for the Advocacy Institute.

Personal and professional characteristics
For this important role, the Advocacy Institute seeks a leader with compelling convictions and vision about the value and purposes of organisations that work for social and economic justice and the importance of developing their leaders. This role demands a broad

array of skills in executive leadership and management. While no one person will possess all of the qualities described below, the ideal candidate would have the following personal and professional characteristics.

Personal qualities

• A passionate commitment to social and economic justice, recognising the importance of developing high quality leaders to forward the agenda of organisations devoted to these causes.

• A management style that is open, collaborative yet results-oriented, and respects the capabilities and independence of staff, while providing them with a clear sense of direction.

• Superb interpersonal skills, with an impressive history of forging strong relationships with multiple constituencies and relating well to people of all backgrounds and at all levels.

• A deep commitment to promoting and supporting a diverse organisation, and an emphasis on diversity in all programming.

• A demonstrated ability to think strategically and plan effectively for an organisation working in a social and economic justice context.

• Excellent written and oral communications skills and an ability to articulate the value of the work of AI to potential funders, the media and the public at large.

• An ability to handle a multitude of tasks simultaneously and to thrive, with grace and humor, under pressure.

• A temperament that is constantly seeking new opportunities and can flourish in a changing environment.

• An aptitude and appetite for fundraising.

Professional experience

• Demonstrated capacity to lead and implement a strategic business plan; adeptness in managing organisational change and seizing opportunities for growth.

• Extensive senior-level non-profit management experience.

• Knowledge of and experience in organising staff around a dynamic strategy and in a changing environment.

- A history of on-the-ground advocacy work, with an experience-based understanding of the dynamics of effective advocacy leadership.

- A demonstrated talent for fundraising, with a track record of substantially increasing philanthropic support for an organisation.

- Direct experience of working with a board of a mission-driven organisation that is actively engaged in the work of the organization.

- A history of successful working relationships with key figures in the advocacy community.

- A track record of leading and developing a dedicated, creative and diverse staff.

- Experience working with advocates outside the United States.

Job Description: Executive Director
Art in Healthcare

Title:	Executive Director
Location:	Edinburgh
Responsible to:	Board of Directors

Art in Healthcare is a progressive arts organisation working with hospital communities to create opportunities for patients, visitors and staff to enjoy and engage with the visual arts. It was formed in 2005 from the charities Paintings in Hospitals Scotland and Friends of Paintings in Hospitals, which provided original works of art for public areas of Scottish hospitals and healthcare units.

Job summary
The Executive Director will continue to develop the forward direction of Art in Healthcare and oversee/manage a small team of part-time staff and volunteers. The position reports to the Board of Directors. The main responsibilities can be categorised as follows:

Development: fundraising and marketing

1. To work with the Board of Directors and the staff to implement and develop the company's Business Plan, and to continue to develop this plan in light of future developments.

2. To devise and implement fundraising and marketing strategies to secure the viability and stability of the organisation and maximise AiH's income and visibility amongst its client-base – i.e. the hospitals, health centres and care homes.

3. To prepare fundraising applications/bids for a wide variety of sources including Charitable Trusts, Scottish Arts Council, local authorities, Lottery, corporate sponsorship and other grant-making groups.

4. To explore new opportunities for the organisation and to develop relationships and partnerships where possible within the healthcare sector, with local authorities, government bodies and arts organisations.

5. To remain informed about developments in arts marketing in the UK.

6. To oversee publicity material, including the production of the Annual Review.

7. To develop opportunities to increase awareness of AiH in the hospital and healthcare sectors.

8. To ensure Art in Healthcare remains competitive and attractive to its various client bases.

9. To undertake research, as necessary, to inform the strategic development of the organisation; to keep informed about developments in arts-in-health, the healthcare sector and arts marketing.

Financial management

1. To ensure good financial practice as defined by the charities law, and to undertake the financial planning of the organisation.

2. To agree both income and expenditure budgets with the Board of Directors and the staff on an annual basis and more frequently if necessary.

3. To regularly monitor and control these agreed budgets in consultation with the staff and report back regularly to the Board of Directors.

4. In association with the arts administrator, to prepare budgets, financial statements, reports, accounts and other financial records as necessary.

Management

1. To pro-actively lead and manage the staff, including support, supervision and monitoring.

2. To determine targets with the staff for all activities and monitor and feedback on their progress and deal with any problems that might arise; and to conduct regular staff performance appraisals.
3. To work with all members of staff to ensure that office and administrative systems work efficiently and effectively. To oversee the maintenance and development of the fundraising database.
4. To ensure that the organisation adheres to good practice in terms of

   - staff contracts
   - welfare and legal employment obligations
   - staff training
   - health and safety
   - equal Opportunities.

   And uphold these policies at all times.
5. To act as Company Secretary for the organisation.
6. To ensure both the care of the collection and the protection of staff.
7. To see that the staff receive training as necessary or appropriate.
8. To organise casual support staff where necessary or appropriate.
9. To abide by, support, implement and develop the organisation's Health and Safety policy, and ensure that the staff and volunteers are trained in and comply with emergency and safety procedures.
10. To ensure effective communication between the staff and the Board of Directors.

Essential skills/experience

- A successful track record of fundraising in a relevant field

- Experience of financial planning

- Strategic management skills including devising and implementing a range of policies

- Staff management experience

- Promotion and advocacy skills, including the ability to forge links with potential funders and partners.

Desirable skills/experience

- Experience of working within an arts organisation

- Awareness of issues surrounding arts-in-health

- Arts marketing experience

- Business/organisational development experience

- Experience working closely with a Board of Directors

- Existing contacts with potential funding organisations within Scotland and/or the UK.

Job Description: Major Gifts Officer
The Trust for Public Land

Position summary

The Major Gifts Officer is responsible for identifying, cultivating, researching, soliciting, and stewarding potential and actual major gift prospects ($100,000+), including planned gifts. Also trains, motivates and manages volunteer leadership with regard to fundraising responsibilities. Other responsibilities include developing programmes, projects, and activities that bring new major donors to TPL, working closely with project and marketing staffs to develop these initiatives, and engaging and training senior regional staff in managing and soliciting current major donors. This position reports to the Regional Director of Development and is responsible for all designated major donors, related campaigns and activities, and volunteers.

Essential functions

- Identifies new individual major donor prospects and develops cultivation, solicitation and stewardship plans to bring these donors into TPL and to renew and increase giving.

- Work with senior staff and volunteers, coordinating the solicitation plans for existing major donors including the establishment of donor follow-up, stewardship, and involvement programmes. Engages existing and new donors in our activities, programmes, and events, implementing and maintaining donor acknowledgement and gift tracking system, making direct solicitations, and coordinating and implementing a planned giving recognition programme.

- Works with project team leaders and other department heads to coordinate and align development activities with other regional priorities and initiatives.

Expectations

- Personally responsible for developing written solicitation plans for new and current major gift donors and prospects managed by MGO.

- Completes 150–200 personal visits per year with donors and prospects.

- Consistently and convincingly demonstrates to colleagues and volunteers the role and importance of charitable giving to TPL.

Qualifications

- Commitment to land conservation.

- Bachelor's degree or equivalent is normally required and a master's degree is preferred.

- 6+ years of development-related experience, including making direct solicitations.

- 2 years of development management experience.

- Excellent communications skills, including oral and written.

- Strong organisational skills and attention to detail.

- Ability to exercise good judgment, take initiative, make recommendations in resolving problems and provide guidance to other staff.

- Experience with PC, including word processing and spreadsheet applications.

- Enthusiastic and good telephone skills.

- Available for travel.

- Knowledge of state funders highly desirable.

CHAPTER NINE

Case Studies

Example isn't another way to teach, it is the only way to teach.
— *Albert Einstein*

The following section is a series of in-depth case studies from eight different organisations. They have been selected to provide a variety of types of causes, geographical locations and size of organisation. Some will be familiar, others you may not have come across. As you will discover, each one approaches major gift fundraising in a slightly different way, making it work for their organisation, which is how we recommend you build your programme.

We hope you will enjoy the lessons that these charities have been willing to generously share with others.

Good luck with your major gift fundraising.

Case Study 1: Major Donor Fundraising at the NSPCC

'A major gift fundraising programme needs to be fully resourced to be effective and this requires a commitment from the trustees and the chief executive. It can't be done by fundraisers alone.'

Background

The Full Stop Campaign laid the foundations for success in major gift fundraising at the NSPCC (National Society for the Prevention of Cruelty to Children), giving it the impetus to develop and invest in this area. The organisation, which provides services in England, Wales and Northern Ireland to end cruelty to children, now has a successful track record in securing major gifts of £100,000 and above.

Critical to its success has been the involvement and role of volunteers. The NSPCC has 21 national and regional committees whose volunteer members drive the major gift fundraising activity. These groups are tasked with either a geographical region or a specific remit, for example one committee fundraises specifically for the NSPCC helpline. One-third of trustees are committee members and most committee members are major donors themselves. This has generated an understanding of major gift fundraising and a supportive culture within each group.

Committees also have explicit terms of reference. Members must give, open networks to other funds, and act as ambassadors for the organisation. Each group must agree an annual fundraising plan, which includes specific prospects and a financial target.

'It takes time to secure significant investment from major donors, therefore major gift fundraising is not about quick wins – it requires a commitment to the long term.'

The committee structure has a bearing upon how prospects are identified. A prospect researcher at the NSPCC will prepare a list of potential prospects from within the networks of the group. The group are then encouraged to add their own at prospect review meetings resulting in about 40 prospects. As a rule, prospects are considered where there is a connection with a member of the group; approaches are therefore rarely cold.

Names are assigned to committee members, and staff then arrange individual follow-up meetings to review the prospects and discuss the opportunity and approach strategy. Each group member reports back at committee meetings on their assigned prospects.

Data relating to the prospect, including propensity and capacity to give, a range for potential value, key opportunities, and other public information about the prospect, are then stored in the fundraising database, Raisers Edge.

For the top prospects with a potential value of £100,000+, internal solicitation meetings take place to consider how to inspire a potential donor to support a specific area of work and create a plan to achieve this.

'The role of the fundraising team is to build the bridges between the donor and the cause and to facilitate the work of volunteer leaders.'

A staff team of 18 manage six of the volunteer groups. They facilitate the work of each committee and support them in delivering the annual plan. The chief executive and other senior and programme staff are also involved, with the chief executive devoting up to 20% of her time to this area of fundraising.

Internally, there is a pervasive appreciation of the importance of voluntary income and the need to protect it: 85% of the charity's income is derived from voluntary sources. Staff therefore understand the value of major donors.

Cultivation

There are a number of engagement events organised annually, but committees also organise their own, incorporating these into their annual plan. Events, which are often dinners, provide an opportunity to learn about the services of the NSPCC and to hear a speaker from a project. Often the discussion results in a brainstorm to generate possible solutions – a technique which is referred to as 'brainstorm dinners'.

There is also a personal testimony from the dinner chair who expresses his or her own commitment and support.

Project visits are used to invite prospects to see the work of the organisation. In an ideal situation, the volunteer committee member is able to join the visit.

Solicitation

A combination of staff and committee members will actually make 'the ask', the invitation to invest in the work of the NSPCC. The staff member will prepare a proposal which will include a precise amount for a specific project. Depending on the individual being asked, the amount of detail in the proposal will vary. However, the proposal might not actually be given to the prospect – it will depend on the conversation. Being flexible and prepared to change the plan for the meeting is key, and staff are trained to use their intuition.

> 'A critical learning point in the solicitation meeting is to motivate the person to want to fund the work. Once "yes" has been achieved you can then worry about the best way to do it by providing examples of how others have funded the work over a period of years. The prospect might need time to think about the "how".'

Recognition for the gift is also discussed and naming opportunities are offered where appropriate.

Once a gift has been made, the ownership of the relationship with the individual is transferred from the volunteer to the staff member who is empowered to maintain the relationship.

Recognition

Staff follow mandatory guidelines on how to acknowledge gifts. The policy includes details such as the procedure for acknowledging cash gifts at various levels, if and how the chairman should be involved, and how to involve the volunteer in the process. This maintains consistency and quality standards in how individuals are thanked across the organisation.

For example, if someone gives at Patron level, they receive a special letter inviting them to become a Patron. If they join, they are given a certificate endorsed by children who receive help from the NSPCC and subsequently receive information on the Patron's own special headed paper (sent in handwritten envelopes with a real stamp). They are also invited to privileged briefings and events, have access to the organisation's leadership, and are the first to be informed about the future of the organisation.

Stewardship

The NSPCC has recently invested in stewarding supporters and has a dedicated team that focuses exclusively on relationship-building, identifying innovative ways of engaging and thanking supporters, and illustrating the impact of the work of the NSPCC. The stewardship team acts as a consultancy team to tailor-make stewardship and deliver bespoke thanks.

The stewardship team consults closely with the fundraisers to identify the best approach. This might include giving a communication to the fundraiser to deliver by hand on a visit.

Stewardship consciously focuses only on recognising, thanking and nurturing supporters. Stewardship programmes are delivered with the aim of applying a consistent approach to how supporters experience the charity. The ultimate goal is to have all of the supporters in a stewardship programme. Every communication is designed to reflect the fact that donors are supporting children and not the NSPCC organisation. For each communication the team asks: What did this project or these funds do for children? How can we bring this to life? How could we make this 'thank you' unique (not just a letter)?

As with many causes, supporters are one step removed from the work of the NSPCC, because it's not often possible to visit or meet the children the organisation supports. The stewardship programme aims to bridge this gap and provide a creative way to engage donors.

Staff are encouraged to be creative; for example, the team put together Christmas parcels for a few special donors which included quotes from children who had benefited from the helpline. The message read, 'Thank you for the best gift you've ever given'.

An annual communications plan is established, but often communication is opportunistic, mixing a formal style with a spur-of-the-moment one. Major donors also receive a certain number of personalised 'high-touch' communications, for example a hand-crafted birthday card from the project they are supporting.

The NSPCC is using stewardship to differentiate the experience donors have of the organisation:

'We want our supporters to have the best experience of giving to a charity.'

Case Study 2: Major Donor Fundraising at The Light Box, Woking

Background

This new gallery and museum in Woking was originally the inspiration of residents in the area. Designed by the creators of the London Eye, Marks Barfield Architects, and featuring stunning materials and spaces, the museum will open in 2007, following a £7 million fundraising campaign. It will offer changing exhibitions covering contemporary art, heritage and local community work; there will be a permanent museum of Woking's history, a café and shop, research facilities, an education studio and spaces for hire. It will bring new cultural opportunities to the region.

The first two years were spent putting the fundraising strategy together and making the case for support and drawing up a major Lottery application. The fundraising drive began in 2002 but the building work did not commence until 2005, when £6.1 million had been raised. The team of three are now raising the last £900K. Major funding has been secured from the Lottery, foundations and the government. It was critical to secure the major statutory funding first, because this gave the project credibility in the community. With the biggest gifts in place, the team have turned their attention to individuals and corporate donors.

> 'Building credibility was part of the strategy so the major statutory funding helped. We received £1.6 million from a Lottery application which took almost a year to work on. A second grant from the Arts Council took a year also. Then we focused on working with trusts which has been successful. We are now doing the high net worth and corporate giving.'

Major donor fundraising began by setting up an appeals committee; new people were mixed with existing trustees who had a fundraising and marketing interest. It began, 'I don't know anyone/thing about fundraising'.

A consultant was hired to undertake a training session and this helped to educate the committee about the fundraising process. The training covered the value of networking, how it's not always the obvious contacts, role-plays for different steps including (a) making the ask – what you do if the person is evasive, and (b) opening the door, for example asking to meet for an informal coffee.

The training proved to be a great success and The Lightbox has seen plenty of evidence of it working in practice; inevitably some committee members are more hands-on than others.

A fundraising administration officer looks after the committee, deals with their appointments, sends them information when they need it, etc.

'Most are very busy people; even if they are retired, they don't have time to address envelopes. Our philosophy is: you tell us what you need and we'll make it happen. They know they'll get a good job done.'

The committee meet every three weeks to download information about the prospects they are working with – and the meeting has an emphasis on action points.

Success story

One supporter gave a costume collection for the museum. The supporter was an elderly lady with known personal wealth. She expressed a desire to make a donation to the museum, but sadly was admitted into a home, her estate was managed by her son and it was unclear how The Lightbox might realise this gift. At a committee meeting, it was discovered that one of the committee members knew her daughter. This volunteer contacted the daughter and explained that her mother had always wanted to give to this project. The volunteer brokered a £50K donation and managed to smooth over what could have been a difficult situation. The team were able to utilise local influential people effectively.

Cultivation

Major donor fundraising was launched with an introductory dinner for 60 people at the historic house of a supporter. The guest list was drawn up from a combination of the appeal committee and names added from research done by the staff. The event provided an introduction to the project.

> 'It wasn't a hard sell – we explained that we were seeking "Founder Sponsors" to fund the project at £10K. During the drinks, we made a presentation outlining the benefits of the project and discussed the architecture of the building itself.'

A member of the appeal committee was present at each table. Their role was to engage people at the table. After the event, a feedback session was held to establish the key prospects and an effective approach strategy. Together with the appeal committee, follow-up meetings were pursued. A member of staff accompanied an appeal committee member to each meeting.

> 'It's better for two people to attend. If you have two people, one can be the more silent and observant, noticing what might perk the interests of a potential donor, while the other can do the talking.'

More often than not, it is not appropriate to make the ask at the first meeting. Instead, this is usually an introductory meeting used to gauge the interest of the prospect. A document is left with the prospect which outlines the benefits of being a Founder Sponsor and a range of gift opportunities ranging from £10K–50K.

Prospect tracking

Approximately 400 prospects are managed on lists in Excel. An 'active' list includes those who have been asked or who are about to be asked and includes people with whom the team have a good connection. The list is reviewed at a weekly meeting to decide what the next action should be. A 'sleeping' list includes those with potential, but where there is no link.

> 'We're always asking ... do you know XYZ with the aim of eventually finding a link.'

The third and fourth lists are 'donors' who have actually given, and 'unsuccessful' is where people are moved to if they respond negatively to an ask. A column tracks what they've been sent.

> 'This type of fundraising works so much better if you can get an introduction. If we can't, we'll eventually cold call.'

Solicitation

'The ask' is led by the committee member. This has ranged from the wife of a medical consultant who wrote to other consultants saying 'I support this' to the story above of the elderly lady who donated her costumes.

> 'The appeals committee don't go anywhere without information on The Lightbox.'

Critical to the success of the fundraising has been building a strong and committed appeals committee. The Lightbox team attribute this to:

• Building the confidence of the individuals involved.

• Dispelling the myth that some are good at fundraising and others aren't, but underscoring that it's a challenge for everyone.

• Building a strong team spirit to encourage them to use each other as sounding boards.

• Creating a sense of ownership of the project and openly sharing its successes and challenges.

Recognition

All donations and donors are sent an acknowledgement in writing from the appropriate appeal committee member and the Director of Development. In addition, every donor will have their name engraved on a glass wall in the building. Larger donors have the opportunity to have a section of the building named after them. Regular communication with donors includes progress reports, site visits and new pictures of the building as it reaches completion.

Case Study 3: Major Donor Fundraising at Capability Scotland

Background

Capability Scotland (CS) is the leading Scottish disability organisation, launched in 1946 by a group of committed parents and professionals. The first service, Westerlea School for children with cerebral palsy, opened in December that year. Originally known as the Scottish Council for Spastics, the organisation became Capability Scotland in 1996.

CS has many long-term, elderly donors and generally receives small gifts on a regular basis. CS has a policy of not fundraising from service users (because of poverty indicators and the fact that this group is less likely to be able to afford to give).

CS started out in major donor fundraising five years ago. It was tortuous at first, with five different databases that needed duplicates eliminated. They began by looking at the size of the gift and the frequency of the gift. They didn't necessarily look for very rich people to consider them as a high-value donor. It was more about loyalty and frequency than gift size.

> 'A high-value donor becomes so at CS based on: size of gift, regularity/frequency of gift, potential to give, longevity (been supporting for a long time). We've developed a matrix to help us identify our high-value donors. Developing these types of tools and creating a good tool-kit which is shared centrally has helped.'

Cultivation

Cultivation at CS includes:

- Keeping close to donors. Make lots of personal visits

- Sending birthday cards to key donors

- CEO writes handwritten postcards to say thank you

- CEO calls them if they are big donors

- Keeping them up-to-date

- Asking them if they want to be acknowledged in the annual report
- Sending pictures of project, where it's at, what's going on.

CS has found that most of its donors don't want recognition. But they all do share CS's vision to ensure that Scotland is treating its disabled people well.

Solicitation

CS has learned that one size does not fit all, because donors are so different. It has used a mixture of staff, the CEO, Director of Fundraising/ Operations but also junior staff who haven't received any formal training to visit donors and make asks.

> 'So much is instinct and common sense – it's about gauging the level of interest.'

Managing across the organisation

The CEO is actively involved in the major gift programme and solicitations. CS holds a CEO lunch annually. The lunch is how the CEO says 'We've selected you as special donors to talk to about our plans'. At the luncheon they will often say 'This time last year, we said X whereas now we can report Y'. It's about making these people feel they have privileged information. We usually have about 20 guests plus senior staff.

> 'We hold the lunch in a boutique hotel and we secure the food and wine for free. It's a working lunch. Everyone is made to feel very special, there is no ask and no pack that people are sent home with. We invite the same people every year and add new people. Anyone who's given over five figures is invited. We also hold a CEO reception once a year at the HQ of the charity. It's the same format as the above.'

The CS staff are very engaged in major donor fundraising because they have responsibility for it and because it is monitored monthly and everyone can see the status. They also have a 'pay-back' scheme to encourage service staff to pass on local potential contacts, where they barter with services to reward them if they identify something that is useful to the fundraising team.

CS has also found that, by sharing information, more service staff feel that they have ownership of the fundraising efforts. The team present their plan to the service staff and say here's how we're going to fundraise, outlining how much is going to be generated from trusts, direct mail, corporate, etc. By taking time to share this information with the service staff, it becomes a joint initiative. It helps to give them the recognition locally through press releases, and CS gets the benefit of the contact. 'Everyone wins; we make the best use of the contact.'

Case Study 4: Major Donor Fundraising at Scope

Background

Scope is a disability organisation in England and Wales whose focus is people with cerebral palsy. The fundraising emphasis is about achieving equality for disabled people and securing funding for new innovative services which can lead to equality. For example, Scope, through a major fundraising campaign which has the working title 'Time to Get Equal 2025', is seeking to secure funding for inclusive education of disabled children in mainstream schools. This involves campaigning to raise awareness about segregated education experienced by disabled children and developing services which lead to their inclusion in mainstream schools. Scope believes that disabled and non-disabled children should be educated in the same schools, as this is where true equality begins. To do this Scope needs an effective strategy and money to develop its bold vision for new inclusive services.

It has developed a new education strategy and is seeking major donors to jointly deliver its outcomes by working directly with the fundraising team.

> 'Our target market is venture philanthropists, major donors who are interested in funding new transformational ventures that will yield a substantial benefit or return. It makes sense for us to target this group as they already seek opportunities to fund bold new ideas for the future.'

Scope is currently in the planning phase of the 'Time to Get Equal 2025' campaign. Major donor fundraising has been part of the fundraising at Scope for several years, although until recently efforts had been *ad hoc*. Scope now aims to achieve a greater market share of the major donor income. A major strategic and cultural change has been taking place at Scope as the organisation seeks to highlight the inequalities disabled people face and develop solutions to current prejudices against them. This has meant that Scope has needed to work with service delivery staff to help cultivate major donors, many of whom are influential in the business sector and have links to other influential individuals. Not all major donors understand Scope's aims and the fundraisers have been at the forefront of creating understanding among influential wealthy people and organisations that have a vested interest in education, equality, human rights and inclusion.

Team structure

Scope has a team of over 20 high-value fundraisers – this includes major donors, trusts, major events and statutory fundraising. It also has a prospect research team of two full-time fundraisers.

> 'We classify donors *new, existing, prospect, or cold*. Our fundraising database reveals their giving history and the nature of our relationship with them to date. Our database allows us to pull off a report on a donor's interest in Scope when we need it. We also look at when donors last gave. Summary points are included on the database. We are now working on identifying major donor suspects and developing research profiles for each donor so that eventually we will be able to hold all our data on Raiser's Edge.'

The fundraising team has set up a 'Time to Get Equal' project team with representation from all areas of the organisation including a trustee, operations, marketing communications, corporate fundraising, trust and major donor, and direct marketing staff. This team is chaired by Scope's Executive Director for External Affairs. They meet regularly to map out the strategy and bring it together as a team, as well as drawing on external consultants for areas where greater expertise is needed, for instance in reaching venture philanthropists who do not yet have contact with the organisation or know about its aspirations for equality and inclusive education.

The major donor fundraising at Scope has an appeal focus. Scope is aiming to raise an as yet undisclosed figure in line with current government plans to achieve equal lives for disabled people in the UK.

> 'Scope doesn't have a traditional base of major donors, like other organisations do, so we've had to start from scratch. We are currently raising about £300K which we are growing, and by 2012 we aim to be raising over £20 million primarily through venture philanthropists and other organisations including companies and trusts.'

The appeal is owned by the executive management board. There has been a deliberate move to bring in senior staff who are change specialists to head up each of the areas of Scope's work. And Scope has been working directly with trustees and 'social investors' who are influential and powerful networks.

Cultivation activities include face-to-face meetings, usually with staff members, and a series of events which range from informal gatherings for a curry to more traditional receptions.

Solicitation

Scope's fundraising style is underpinned by a commitment to respect the dignity and fundamental right of disabled people to be portrayed not as 'handicapped', but as 'equal', citizens. This means fundraisers often have to explain Scope's mission and vision by showing what equality really means and tapping into the things that make donors tick – such as wanting to make a difference and being associated with a powerful transformational cause. There are many opportunities for donors to receive recognition for their support of Scope, either as a trustee or a patron. Quite often fundraisers mould the project pitch to the donors' interests and attention areas. However, fundraisers can also be at the forefront of changing a donor's own negative attitudes and this is done in a very sensitive way over a period of time.

> 'Inclusive education is one of the major projects we're developing. Not enough disabled children have the opportunity to have a mainstream education. Our job is to paint the end goal which involves a future where disabled and non-disabled children are educated in the same schools. It's the end goal that grips people and challenges their perceptions. We need them to think: 'this is my project – no one has done it worldwide' – that's the draw to this type of donor. We paint the picture that this project will provide one almighty opportunity to change the world through one of Scope's transformational services. The journey Scope's major donors are taken through is often enlightening, life-changing and fun.'

When meeting with a major donor for the first time, Scope fundraisers often take some Scope 'Time to Get Equal' branded documents, such as Scope's Research produced in conjunction with the think-tank 'Demos', and information about Scope services. Where appropriate, the team will also use branded light-hearted props including desk toys and t-shirts as an ice-breaker which helps to create a light-hearted situation initially before discussing serious issues.

Scope has also developed a powerful CD ROM featuring its work and supporters. It highlights how society disadvantages disabled people, using real life situations which form part of the discussion with the major donor.

Case Study 5: Major Donor Fundraising at the London School of Economics and Political Science

Background

The London School of Economics and Political Science (LSE) was founded in 1895 and is a centre for the concentration of teaching and research across the full range of the social, political, and economic sciences. The School's fundraising activities have developed over the last 14 years to the extent that today there is a developed major gift programme and a wide appreciation of its importance.

There are a number of differences between a typical charity and university fundraising. First, universities have advantages, such as a history and a defined audience through their alumni because of pre-existing relationships. Second, many charities raise funds on an annual basis, which has a rhythm that is different from major gift fundraising. Major gift fundraising requires much longer lead times and a shift from dealing with donors in volume, which not every charity can afford to do.

The LSE has adopted a disciplined and strategic approach to major-gift fundraising. The following steps are considered critical to the process of planning and securing major gifts:

- Research
- Cultivation
- Solicitation
- Acknowledgement
- Stewardship.

Research

In addition to major gift officers, the LSE has a full-time researcher who focuses on researching LSE alumni, many of whom have become lost contacts over time.

> 'In the UK, alumni don't have the sense of affiliation with their college that exists in the US. There's a mentality in Britain that you don't look back. There is no sense of class identification with a particular year.'

Major gift research at the LSE is focused on initially identifying prospective donors with financial capacity, using traditional and electronic media. Once these individuals have been identified, further research is done to learn as much as possible about the prospective donors, including factors such as their interests, careers, and networks.

Cultivation

The major gifts programme is about discipline, *making consistent calls and personal visits*, which are the engine of the programme. It is during these visits that an individual's propensity – perhaps the most important determinant in philanthropy – is assessed. Gift officers have a target number of visits to achieve over the year. Half of the alumni are overseas; a major gift officer therefore visits specified countries. The LSE's database is essential.

'We can pull out a portfolio of prospects or run a report at any time. If you did this without using a database, you'd guarantee that the list wouldn't be complete. A good prospect tracking system in your database is essential.'

Central to good data management is a commitment to documenting all interactions with donors. Call reports are produced after each visit or interaction with a prospective donor and serve as the historical record documenting the organisation's (not the fundraiser's) relationship with the prospect. The School now has consistency of practice and good record keeping, which have only been achieved after many years of implementing these practices.

Fundraising staff capitalise on existing programme activities at the School to re-engage alumni back into the life of the LSE, as well as creating them. The LSE organises reunions and uses the School's extensive lecture series, which has been very attractive to donors. Staff also arrange lunches with academics.

'We also have a high-level campaign committee who are volunteers. This group is a subset of the board with a remit to help with our appeal. They are people who have given gifts previously. For major gift fundraising, this group sets the terms of generosity for others.'

This group of influential and committed volunteers serves in a variety of capacities, including hosting private – and exclusive – events in their homes or at other venues, providing an opportunity to elevate prospects. Increasingly, they are becoming involved in one-to-one solicitations.

Solicitation

> 'Our job is to engage donors. When you are persuading people to give, they need to understand that they can make the difference. Don't talk about money first – money isn't the driver – the mission is the driver and private philanthropy is the fuel.'

The goal of solicitation is to maximise the donor's philanthropic interest. Often, the key to achieving this is to ensure that the 'right people are in the room' to make the request. The LSE often uses a two-person asking team. For high-level prospects who warrant a personal request from the CEO, the School's Director leads the request. Other asks are made by staff, academics, or volunteers, and always after careful analysis to identify the best approach and cooperation with the fundraising team. The LSE has also found it effective to take donors to meet with prospects, and that success typically increases when a donor says, 'I gave, and I'd like you to join me.'

During face-to-face meetings, a success factor has been to make a point of listening to what is of interest to the donor. The LSE does not provide a list of options, but rather discovers the interests of the donor by listening for what matters most and makes the closest match with the School's priorities. Then it makes a recommendation, saying, 'I'd like to get back to you with a proposal for £X at £X gift range.'

To maximise gifts, the staff and volunteers need to be well-versed in the organisation's priorities and in the mechanics of making a gift. For instance, knowledge about the fiscal benefits of gifts of shares and taking advantage of Gift Aid have been critical in assisting donors to increase their generosity to the School. Staff do not replace the role of the tax adviser or accountant but need to have the financial acumen to make suggestions that will benefit both the donor and the organisation.

Acknowledgement

The key to developing a strong continuing relationship with donors is to express gratitude – regularly, appropriately, and with great accountability. The organisation should provide as much transparency about the use and purpose of the gift as possible. All gifts are acknowledged at least once. Naming opportunities are offered for major gifts.

The LSE has carefully crafted its acknowledgement programme that is designed around the type and purpose of each gift. For example, a gift for a building would result in a report on the gift, an invitation for the donors to meet with the architects, and a recognition event. For scholarships, the acknowledgements include a letter from the student and an annual lunch with them.

The LSE's recognition programme is included in the gift agreement with donors. This way, the donor's expectations are managed effectively.

The LSE's gift agreement includes:

- what the donor will give
- the use of the gift
- the schedule of payments
- how the gift will be recognised.

Stewardship

'When setting guidelines, consider the size of gift for a certain kind of recognition. You need to be consistent – or donors will discover you are treating them differently. If a professorship is £2m, you don't want the donor to find out that another donor secured one for less.'

The best cultivation occurs when a donor is brought into the fabric of the School. To this end, LSE development staff are fortunate. The academic reputation of the School and its desire to remain in the forefront of academic and policy discourse provide many opportunities for events and other occasions in which donors may be involved.

The leadership shown by the Director (Vice Chancellor) has also been a critical component of success. The involvement of volunteer and staff leadership in relationship-building with donors is not to be underestimated and often makes the difference between modest and significant major gift successes.

In addition, the development office is committed to creating appropriate opportunities to engage donors and prospects in the life of the School as part of its stewardship activity. The alumni staff have worked hard to create a worldwide network of local alumni clubs. Fundraising staff regularly ensure that benefactors see the results of their largesse, whether to students, academics, or buildings.

All of these activities aid the continuing collection of information about an individual's capacity and propensity to give. This, of course, leads back to increased research. The cycle is initiated once again as plans commence for the donor's next major gift.

Case Study 6: Major Donor Fundraising at the CancerBACKUP

Background

CancerBACKUP (CB) was founded in 1985 and its mission is to give cancer patients and their families the up-to-date information, practical advice and support they need to reduce the fear and uncertainty of cancer. The major donor programme at CB is two years old. When it was first set up, it failed because of a lack of relationship-management. The 21st birthday of the charity was a milestone for the programme.

At CB a major donor gives £10K or above. The programme currently manages about 15–16 people. We know that a great many of our donors are also our service users. They are looking at new ways of reaching new groups of people.

The major gift programme began with two major donors who wanted to support CB, so they developed the 'Benefactors Scheme' under which each donor gives £10K a year for three years, specifically to raise funds to cover the costs of a cancer nurse.

A chairman was secured for the scheme and began networking to find others with similar interests. Some of the benefactors are giving £10K each year, others have raised £25K per year. The club includes both those who give from their own personal wealth and those who commit to raising the funds by whatever means. They've supported events, fundraised in their own right and raised the money. Being part of the Benefactor's Scheme elevates them and they receive specific recognition through being part of the group.

Benefactors receive a special quarterly newsletter that is focused on outlining how the money is spent and the difference it makes. There are updates on advocacy so this group knows first-hand what CB is doing with the government and that makes them feel that it is very private and privileged information.

Cultivation

In terms of relationship-building, each major donor prospect has their own plan. Each person is thoroughly researched, Google alerts are set up on individual names to look at how people can be matched up with the work that CB is doing.

'We organise project visits, inviting them to spend time with the CEO. We will send them updates by newsletter. If they phone and say, "Please can you send so and so", we'll make sure that it is done quickly and we'll keep them in touch with the result.'

Mid-level donor prospects come through the direct mail programme. The CB development staff clusters those who are making a higher-level gift within the programme and takes a look at each one. Their approach is very much about working with individuals and their networks. The result is finding people who are moving in the same circles.

Door-opening strategies that CB uses include phone calls direct from our CEO. 'One needs to make sure that one is not precious about the contact – it's better to find the right person to develop the relationship.' They also arrange for a lunch or breakfast with the CB chairman as a way of getting in the door. They also ask other people who know the donor to help them through their endorsement of CB's work.

Solicitation

The development team uses the seven steps of solicitation to manage major donors. In terms of identifying new prospects, they often find new ones from their trustees or chairman, who are then researched.

The CEO is very involved and the CB chairman has significant networks. 'Our chair will often raise a potential new contact with our CEO. Our CEO likes to make the initial phone call to approach the contact and will invite them in for a meeting. When they come in, they'll be given a brief tour and shown the helpline in action.'

Acknowledgement

CB major donors are coded into three categories according to their giving history.

Bronze:	£500–£2K
Silver:	£2–5K
Gold:	£5K+

Once they are in any of these categories, they get treated differently in terms of intensity of information, appreciation and respect. They get more attention, the larger their gift(s).

'When thanking donors, who thanks depends on how much they've given and on who has the relationship with them. We will often place a thank-you phone call. We'll also send a letter of thanks. Sometimes we'll send a card, not a letter. We also hold thank-you receptions. We hold one a year. We also use our trustees – having people on our board invite people in to our cultivation/thank-you events.'

Stewardship

Stewardship is important, one needs to make sure that these donors are getting the right kind of attention and one also needs to know what might make them tick. Some of them might want to meet HRH or maybe simply have lunch with the chairman. 'You need to be aware all the time of their interests.'

Case Study 7: Major Donor Fundraising at Friends of the Earth

Friends of the Earth is an international environmental charity committed to the conservation, protection and improvement of the environment. The charity undertakes independent research and provides extensive information and education resources, including a public information service. Services are designed to inform people about the threats to the environment so that they can take appropriate steps to protect and conserve, democratically and peacefully.

The current major gift programme was established six years ago and is currently raising £1.2 million each year. The team manages a portfolio of approximately 600 prospects and stewards 120 major donors, made up of a mixture of individuals and trusts.

Research

The prospect research function is outsourced to a research agency that identifies potential new donors from the Friends of the Earth database and undertakes in-depth profiles as required. This is supplemented by research done in-house, particularly looking at people who may have publicly shown an interest in a cause in the media. New prospects are also identified using financial triggers – i.e. if they make a gift of £500 or £1K cumulatively or if they make a generous gift (more than they were asked for) – and after being profiled they are identified as having the capacity to give more than £5K.

Once a prospect has been identified, information about the individual is added to the database and donors are coded according to their giving potential, warmth towards the organisation, and 'fit' to the cause. The database also serves to record all future interactions between the organisation and the donor.

Researching an individual's networks and contacts has been effective and has resulted in a number of successful applications being made through personal approaches to trustees of major foundations.

Cultivation

Cultivation activities include an annual programme of two dinners, one seminar and several special lunches. Dinners are small (just six to eight guests) and intimate; lunches are also small but more informal; and seminars are briefing events for a larger audience. All are themed on a particular topic such as climate change or food and farming. The purpose of these events is to invite both existing donors and new prospects to learn more about the work of the organisation.

'The format is a speech from the CEO followed by a brief talk about our work from the Head of Campaigns. Guests and other relevant staff are also invited to speak.'

All events are planned with meticulous detail. Senior staff attend and are 'matched' to donors, depending on the donor's interests. They will have specific information to find out about the individuals attending. In some cases they will also be briefed to ask the CEO a specific question that the team wants the audience to hear. Donors are also invited where appropriate to events taking place outside of the major donor programme – for example, parliamentary briefings – if the topic is of interest to the donor.

Solicitation

Friends of the Earth insists from experience that a face-to-face meeting is essential. The meeting involves two or three staff, carefully selected based on knowledge of the donor, usually including the CEO or the head of campaigns, a campaigner and a major gift fundraiser. The role of the fundraiser is to ensure that the purpose of the meeting is achieved; occasionally this may mean being prepared to step in to make the ask, although this is usually done by the CEO. The fundraiser is also prepared to discuss the fiscal benefits of Gift Aid or making a tax-efficient gift.

A high-level advocacy programme has recently been established to support the major-donor fundraising function and to develop peer-to-peer solicitations. Friends of the Earth found that it needed to be flexible as high-level volunteers were not prepared to sign up to the formality of a job description and specific task. However, they were prepared to sign up to involvement in the programme: opening up their address book and making introductions to key individuals, supporting funding applications, advocating to others and championing the cause.

'Donors did not want the formality of being "public advocates" but were still prepared to do everything that we asked of them.'

Friends of the Earth aims to be transparent and is explicit about the ask when requesting a meeting. This is usually done by letter or telephone.

Stewardship and donor care

Donors are made to feel they are on the inside track and receive privileged information before others; for example, staff will distribute a report to major donors before it is published.

Regular communication is maintained through email news alerts which are personalised, as many donors prefer to receive email because it is more environmentally friendly. Staff will also send copies of recent news coverage in the media and regular written programme updates, or make calls to update the donor. A report is distributed every six months highlighting key achievements and providing an account of how funds have been spent, and staff aim to meet face-to-face with all major donors at least once a year.

An emphasis is placed on providing a preferential service: envelopes are always handwritten, letters are hand signed.

The staff have found that they need to be very well briefed on the work of Friends of the Earth and need to be able to speak on a wide range of issues at any time.

'We might have a donor at any minute call us and say, "What do you think about XX? And what is FOE doing about Y issue?" It's a challenge because I'm not a campaigns specialist and we are a complex organisation.'

This has also worked in reverse and a series of days have been organised to educate the wider organisation about the role, practice and function of major gift fundraising.

The strategies employed are reaping rewards for Friends of the Earth. One donor who was identified in the direct marketing database was cultivated over a period of several years. Initially invited to events, but always unable to attend, the donor finally attended a dinner in 2002. After the dinner a thank-you letter and a donation of £1K was received. A follow-up meeting resulted in a donation of £10K, followed a year later by a gift of £100K.

Friends of the Earth then sent reports, press clippings and made regular phone calls with reports about what we were doing, and over a period of time have developed this relationship so that we now receive £75K per year.

Case Study 8: Major Gift Fundraising at the British Heart Foundation

Major donor fundraising has existed formally at BHF since 2002. In 2004, the BHF launched a major donor club and a £2 million appeal.

Direct marketing and event fundraising have featured prominently in the programme. A direct mail pack was specifically developed to attract £1K+ donors. The pack is mailed to warm supporters and cold prospects with a capacity to give at this level. Recipients are invited to join the unique donor club – and to learn more about the work of BHF. A major annual dinner also supports the appeal.

Currently BHF has 70 donors, with a target to recruit 100 to support one professor undertaking research into heart disease in children under the age of 10.

The major projects fundraising department currently has six staff and focuses on major donors, trusts and statutory funding. Its purpose is to identify major BHF projects and to match them to appropriate major funders. A key objective of the department is to establish high-level net-working throughout the BHF to maximise income.

The Ranulph Fiennes Healthy Hearts Appeal

BHF has structured its major donor fundraising around an appeal called the Healthy Hearts Appeal which aims to raise £2 million to fund an MRI scanner and a catheter laboratory for the Heart Hospital and Institute of Child's Health at Great Ormond Street. The focus of the appeal is research into children with heart disease.

The structure of the appeal is two-tiered: to secure major gifts through a committee (and their networks) and to generate funds through direct marketing initiatives. Sir Ranulph Fiennes is heading up the appeal as its Chairman.

Ranulph Fiennes attempted to climb the North Face of Mount Everest at the beginning of June 2005, but chest pains forced him to abandon the attempt 300 metres from the summit. Sir Ranulph suffered a heart attack and had a double heart bypass operation in 2003. He is a committed ambassador for the BHF.

Since November 2004 the appeal has raised £1.8 million. Donations have been generated from a variety of sources including a very large dona-tion from a leading figure who sponsored Sir Ranulph's ascent of Mt Everest. Following his climb, a dinner was held in Sir Ranulph's honour which raised £100K for the appeal and was supported by the appeal committee who helped to secure tables. Notably, the committee and their networks have generated 75% of the appeal income.

The committee meet every few months either in person or by con-ference calls. The agenda includes a review of their prospects, other new donors and prospects, new club members and a discussion about who to target for project visits.

The committee have been doing most of the 'asks'. Some are more active than others due to time constraints. The role of the fundraising team is to facilitate their efforts and report on progress.

> 'We prepare letters, do the groundwork for them, and staff follow up some of our warmer donors (£1K–5K). The committee focus their energy on securing gifts of £5K+.'

Research

Prospect research is done in-house by the team and by excellent volunteers, although most leads are generated through the committee. There is no dedicated prospect researcher. A template prospect profile form helps to organise the research data.

Useful resources include a subscription to MINT – a subscription business intelligence database which gives access to a wide range of high quality information covering companies, news, directors and market research – Debretts and the internet.

Internal coordination involves a regular meeting to review the prospect list and reports on income generated from Raiser's Edge.

Cultivation

Cultivation activities include private dinners and business breakfasts, usually hosted by the chair or another member of the committee. These events rely heavily on the host inviting his or her warm contacts. A professor whose work is being funded is invited to talk about the programme.

Contact with major prospects is maintained quarterly through a range of other activities including project visits to the Institute of Child Health at Great Ormond Street, the annual dinner and renewal letters. The team want to do more personal visits to ensure that they find a way of engaging people in future appeals.

> 'Being part of the appeal itself makes people feel part of it; we need to communicate the ongoing successes. Site visits have been very successful and this also depends on having a good relationship with the professors. They have been great. We need to treat them like our major donors too, keeping them engaged, keeping them informed, not overloading them and allowing the relationship to develop over time.'

Stewardship

New donors receive a welcome call and thank you letter. Significant donations also receive a personal letter from the Director General. The correspondence is kept very personal and is recognisably special.

Future emphasis will be placed on doing less mass direct marketing and focusing more on identifying quality names and undertaking personalised approaches. In addition, retention is being addressed and the BHF are identifying mechanisms to involve these supporters in future appeals.

'One of the challenges we're addressing is how we keep our major supporters engaged longer-term. There are only so many dinners you can do. We're looking at other ways currently.'

Glossary of terms

Capacity An assessment of an individual's financial capacity to make a gift, based on an estimation of net-worth including factors such as income, life-stage and assets.

Connection An association or link between a prospect and someone connected to your organisation. For example, a trustee or volunteer who is a business associate, neighbour or friend of the prospect.

Cultivation A planned sequence of activities designed to build a relationship with a prospect and engage them in the work of the organisation.

Development board A committee of volunteers with a specific remit to raise funds for the organisation.

Face-to-face ask A request for financial support made in person, usually by a volunteer or trustee who has given at a similar level and a representative from the organisation.

Friend-raising A term used to describe the process of developing a relationship with a prospect, also known as cultivation.

Interest A subjective assessment of the level of interest a prospect has in a cause/organisation. Indicators might include previous gift history, frequency of interaction, attendance at an event, previous support of a similar cause, or a member of the family with a connection to your cause.

Major gift club A dedicated programme of activity designed to facilitate annual gifts at above-average levels. Also described as a patron, recognition society, or high-level giving club; gift clubs provide a mechanism for acknowledging, publicising, and celebrating donors who make a continuing commitment to your cause.

Model One Organisation A small organisation with no major donor base and only one or two staff members.

Model Two Organisation A mid-sized organisation with a few major gift donors and some connections to high-profile individuals or celebrities often through special events. These charities may have a fundraising director, or the chief executive is the fundraiser.

Model Three Organisation A mid-sized organisation with a classic appeals committee that helps the staff identify, solicit and steward major donors. These charities have both a chief executive and a fundraising director involved with fundraising.

Moves Management® A tool developed by two Americans, David Dunlop and GT 'Buck Smith, at Cornell University to organise and systemise *meaningful* contacts with donors and prospects. Moves Management® enables a fundraiser to cluster prospects with the greatest potential, as well as track 'moves' that draw the prospect closer to an organisation.

Narrative philanthropy The ability to express a charity's mission to a prospective donor in your own words, using descriptive stories that paint a picture of the charity's accomplishments and goals.

Net worth A compilation of an individual's total assets, including stock and real estate holdings, annual salary, and retirement plan assets.

Network research Using research tools, including the internet, to develop networks of prospects that are linked to the charity and the charity's board.

Peer screening A series of confidential meetings where board members and others gather to discuss the capacity and propensity of major gift prospects to make a large gift.

Peer-to-peer ask When a person who moves in the same social or business circles, who has given approximately the same amount or more, asks a colleague or friend for a gift.

Propensity to give An individual's willingness or readiness to make a gift that is based on a perception by the charity of the donor's closeness and/or interest in the charity's mission.

Prospect An individual who has been identified as a potential donor to a charity.

Prospect screening A series of activities undertaken by the development office to identify an individual's ability and propensity to make a major gift. This often involves assigning the prospect a capacity and propensity-to-give rating.

Recognition society A programme to acknowledge and steward donors on a regular basis. These societies often include a listing in the charity's publications, events, small tokens of appreciation, special visits, and other personalised communications.

Return on Investment (ROI) A performance measure used to evaluate the efficiency of an investment or to compare the efficiency of a number of different investments. To calculate ROI, the benefit (return) of an investment is divided by the cost of the investment; the result is expressed as a percentage or a ratio.

Solicitation The process of asking a prospect or donor for a gift.

Stewardship A programme to systematically continue to strengthen a relationship with a donor. This may include frequent communication, meetings, and invitations to events.

Suspect An individual whose ability to make a major gift or interest level in the charity is unknown.

Time value of money The time value of money is based on the premise that one will prefer to receive a certain amount of money today rather than the same amount in the future, all else being equal. Money received today is more valuable than money received in the future by the amount of interest the money can earn. If £90 today will accumulate to £100 a year from now, then the *present* value of £100 to be received one year from now is £90.

Volunteer leadership Volunteers have a wealth of knowledge and personal experiences to share, and come to an organisation understanding the mission of that organisation. A quality volunteer leader is one who acts as an ambassador for the organisation and who shares the same sense of mission and direction, and feels conviction and a commitment to the organisation.

Other publications from the Directory of Social Change

DSC is the leading provider of information and training for the voluntary sector. It publishes an extensive range of guides, handbooks, and CD-ROMs, covering subjects such as fundraising, management, communication, finance and law.

Call 08450 777707 or e-mail publications@dsc.org.uk for more details and for a free publications catalogue. You can also view and order online at the DSC website (www.dsc.org.uk).

The fundraising series

Published in association with CAF and the Institute of Fundraising.

Capital Campaigns
Trudy Hayden

Capital campaigns require precisely defined, tightly structured fundraising strategies that can radically improve the fundraiser's chances of success, yet smaller organisations often lack the resources to hire specialists to manage their campaigns for them. This new guide gives the fundraiser, the CEO, the trustees and other management staff the information necessary to run a successful capital campaign – with or without a consultant's input.

Drawing upon her experience planning and managing several highly visible and successful campaigns, the author first defines what a capital campaign is, before going through each stage of their preparation and execution, including:

- the decision to run a campaign
- establishing goals for your campaign
- preparing strategies
- post-campaign tactics.

128 pages, 1st edition, 2006, ISBN 1 903991 62 5

Community Fundraising
Edited by Harry Brown

Volunteer networks are a key resource for fundraising, but are often not appreciated as they should be. This new title demonstrates how to make the most of your volunteers. It covers:

- what community fundraising is
- why people volunteer, the value of volunteers and staff attitudes to volunteers
- the recruitment, retention and development of volunteers
- the management of staff working with volunteers
- case studies from a range of different types of charities – and what can be learned from these.

192 pages, 1st edition, 2002 ISBN 1 900360 98 5

Corporate Fundraising
Edited by Valerie Morton

Corporate Fundraising is a fast-moving area and the second edition of this book has been completely revised and updated to include:

- new chapters on corporate social responsibility and on evaluation
- a new appendix on the internet
- a revised section on the legal and tax framework
- a range of new case studies from major charities and companies such as NCH, Diabetes UK, One2One and the Mencap–Transco partnership.

The book continues to offer a comprehensive overview, detailing the variety of ways in which charities and companies may work together to mutual advantage, and addressing key issues around ethics and standards.

200 pages, 2nd edition, 2002 ISBN 1 903991 00 5

Fundraising Databases
Peter Flory

Computerised databases are an essential tool for fundraising, but fundraisers often lack the technical background to help them choose a suitable database and use it effectively. This book provides a clear framework for making and implementing such decisions. It explains what a database is and how it works, before going on to examine:

- why fundraisers need a database
- the functions of a fundraising database
- future trends.

Case studies from a range of charities are used throughout to illustrate the points made.

160 pages, 1st edition, 2001 ISBN 1 900360 91 8

Fundraising Strategy
Redmond Mullin

The key to successful fundraising is rigorous strategic planning and this influential title has become essential reading for all serious fundraisers, as a background to the whole series. The second edition draws on some more recent examples, such as the NSPCC Full Stop campaign, to further clarify the principles and process of strategy and demonstrate its place in fundraising campaigns. The book:

- discusses the concept of strategy and its relevance to not-for-profit bodies
- outlines the planning process for designing and implementing the strategy
- provides case studies of different strategies in different types and sizes of funding programmes
- has been fully updated to take into account important changes in areas such as the tax regime and the National Lottery.

160 pages, 2nd edition, 2002 ISBN 1 903991 22 6

Legacy Fundraising
The Art of Seeking Bequests
Edited by Sebastian Wilberforce

This unique guide to one of the most important sources of revenue for charities has been revised and updated to include new material on telephone fundraising, forecasting income, and profiling. It also contains the full text of the new Institute of Fundraising Code of Practice on legacy fundraising. Contributions from a range of experts in the field cover both strategy and techniques, and are complemented by perspectives from donors and their families. The breadth of coverage and accessible style ensure that, whether you are an established legacy fundraiser or new to the field, this book is a must.

224 pages, 2nd edition, 2001 ISBN 1 900360 93 4

Trust Fundraising
Edited by Anthony Clay

This book outlines a variety of approaches to trusts that will save trustees' time and ensure greater success for fundraising by:

- emphasising the importance of research and maintaining records
- demonstrating the value of using contacts and a personal approach
- reinforcing the need for detailed planning of a strategy
- showing how to make an approach to trusts, and how not to
- stressing the importance of continued contact with a trust.

152 pages, 1st edition, 1999 ISBN 1 85934 069 5

Other fundraising titles from DSC

DSC publishes s a range of other fundraising titles, including both directories and practical guides. Biannual directories include *A Guide to the Major Trusts* (volumes 1 and 2), *The Educational Grants Directory*, *The Guide to Grants for Individuals in Need* and *The Guide to UK Company Giving*. All titles can be ordered online (www.dsc.org.uk/charitybooks. html) or by calling 08450 77 77 07.

We also host three subscription-based fundraising websites: *trustfunding.org. uk*, *grantsforindividuals.org.uk* and *companygiving.org.uk*. Information is taken from all the major directories, and is constantly updated.

About CAF

CAF, Charities Aid Foundation, is a registered charity with a unique mission – to increase the substance of charity in the UK and overseas. It provides services that are both charitable and financial which help donors make the most of their giving and charities make the most of their resources.

As an integral part of its activities, CAF works to raise standards of management in voluntary organisations. This includes the making of grants by its own Grants Council, sponsorship of the Charity Annual Report and Accounts Awards, seminars, training courses and its own Annual Conference, the largest regular gathering of key people from within the voluntary sector. In addition, CAF is recognised as a leading exponent of the internet for all those with an interest in charitable activity.

For decades, CAF has led the way in developing tax-effective services to donors, and these are now used by more than 250,000 individuals and 2,000 of the UK's leading companies, between them giving £150 million each year to charity. Many are also using CAF's unique range of investment and administration services for charities includes the CafCash High Interest Cheque Account, three specialist investment funds for longer-term investment and a full appeals and subscription management service.

CAF's activities are not limited to the UK, however. Increasingly, CAF is looking to apply the same principles and develop similar services internationally, in its drive to increase the substance of charity across the world. CAF has offices and sister organisations in the United States, South Africa, Russia, India and Brussels.

CAF Research is a leading source of information and research on the voluntary sector's income and resources. Its annual publication, *Dimensions of the Voluntary Sector*, provides year-on-year updates and its Research Report series covers a wide range of topics, including costs benchmarking, partnership resources, and trust and company funding. More details on research and publications may be found on www.CAFonline.org/research

For more information about CAF, please visit www.CAFonline.org/

About IOF

The Institute of Fundraising (IOF) is the professional membership body for fundraisers, working to develop, promote and champion excellence in UK fundraising. Committed to the highest standards in fundraising practice and management, the Institute is the leading representative voice for fundraising. It works to shape policy and influence legislation, engaging with charities, Government, media, the general public, and other relevant bodies across a broad spectrum of issues that impact UK fundraising.

The Institute strives to support and develop the knowledge and standards of all those who undertake fundraising and has developed an extensive range of training and networking opportunities. The Institute's Certificate in Fundraising Management is the leading qualification for fundraisers and is delivered by accredited training providers across the country.

The Institute offers an extensive programme of events across the country. The flagship event, the National Convention, is the largest fund-raising event of its type outside the USA, attracting around 2,000 charity representatives of all levels. The comprehensive three-day programme is supplemented by a series of targeted one-day fundraising conferences taking place throughout the year.

As a membership body, the Institute represents over 4,000 fundraisers and 200 fundraising organisations, providing a wide range of informa-tion and support services for Individual and Organisational members. Individual membership supports fundraisers in providing practical tools that help them fundraise more effectively, opportunities to share and discuss common issues, as well as professional development support and advice. Organisational membership is an organisation-wide commitment to best practice in fundraising and provides a fast-track route to effect change in the UK fundraising environment.

Membership benefits include a free subscription to *Third Sector* magazine, the Codes of Fundraising Practice, a monthly email briefing covering key fundraising issues, access to a free legal helpline (provided by Bircham Dyson Bell), substantial discount packages on training and networking events, and more.

The Institute is represented across the UK by a range of national, regional and special-interest groups.

The Codes of Fundraising Practice and Code of Conduct

The Institute of Fundraising's Codes of Fundraising Practice set out the best practice standards for fundraisers operating within the UK. Each Code covers a separate fundraising technique or issue, as well as an overarching Code of Conduct setting out the framework of ethical behaviour for fundraisers. The Codes provide not only information on relevant areas of the law but outline recommended practice based upon the highest standards of fundraising.

All 4,000 Individual and 200 Organisational members of the Institute have already committed to meet the best practice guidance outlined within the Code. The Codes are the best practice criteria upon which the forthcoming self-regulatory scheme for fundraising is built.

The Codes are drawn up by working parties composed of representatives of the various interested constituents in a particular field, and undergo an extensive consultation process through the charities affiliated with the Institute of Fundraising, regulators and Government. As new areas of interest are identified, so new Codes are drafted, under the supervision of the Institute of Fundraising Standards Committee.

The Codes of Fundraising Practice cover the following areas:

- Acceptance and Refusal of Donations
- Best Practice for Fundraising Contracts
- Best Practice for Major Donor Fundraising
- Charities Working with Business
- Charity Challenge Events
- Committed Giving in the Workplace
- Event Fundraising
- Fundraising from Grant Making Trusts
- Fundraising in Schools
- Fundraising through Electronic Media

- Handling Cash Donations
- House to House Collections
- Legacy Fundraising
- Management of Static Collection Boxes
- Outdoor Fundraising Events in the UK
- Payment of Fundraisers on a Commission Basis
- Personal Solicitation for Committed Gifts
- Raffles and Lotteries
- Reciprocal Charity Mailings
- Scottish Charity Law in Relation to Fundraising and Public Charitable Collections in Scotland
- Telephone Fundraising
- Telephone Recruitment of Collectors
- Use of Chain Letters as a Fundraising Technique
- Volunteer Fundraising

For more information:

Institute of Fundraising
Park Place
12 Lawn Lane
London
SW8 1UD

Tel: 020 7840 1000
Fax: 020 7840 1001

Email: enquiries@institute-of-fundraising.org.uk
Web: www.institute-of-fundraising.org.uk

The Institute of Fundraising is a Registered Charity no. 1079573 and a company Limited by Guarantee no. 3870883. VAT Registration no. 547 8930 96.

Index